Joy in the Fire

To my brother in Christ —
Derrick Roberts —

May the Lord continue to
bless the works of your hands
and guide your footsteps.
Be Blessed —

Sis Bryant
7/6/17

Joy in the Fire

✦

My Love Of Catherine

Denise F. Bryant

iUniverse, Inc.
New York Lincoln Shanghai

Joy in the Fire
My Love Of Catherine

iUniverse books may be ordered through booksellers or by contacting:

iUniverse
2021 Pine Lake Road, Suite 100
Lincoln, NE 68512
www.iuniverse.com
1-800-Authors (1-800-288-4677)

Senior Editor, Publishing Services: Cynthia Lowery-Ford
Cover Design: Denise F. Bryant & Cynthia Lowery-Ford
Cover Layout & Design: CLF Enterprises
Cover Art Enhancement: iUniverse A portion of the proceeds from the sale of this Book is being donated to the: CATHERINE HUNT FOUNDATION, INC.

ISBN-13: 978-0-595-36766-5 (pbk)
ISBN-13: 978-0-595-67415-2 (cloth)
ISBN-13: 978-0-595-81185-4 (ebk)
ISBN-10: 0-595-36766-6 (pbk)
ISBN-10: 0-595-67415-1 (cloth)
ISBN-10: 0-595-81185-X (ebk)

Printed in the United States of America

TO

James Eric Hunt
and
Katrina Louise Hunt

In memory of all those who lost their life unnecessarily in nursing homes through all America.

It is hoped that you who have experienced abusive childhoods or lost loved ones due to an unfortunate situation will see good from it.

Pathways

Acknowledgements

At some point, through all the trials and tribulations, there must come a time to say,

Thank you! The success and continuance of the bill to remain "alive" belongs to the various organizations, groups, and individuals. Their unselfish efforts, time, and experience have contributed to improving the quality of life for nursing home residents through all the United States.

Thank you to my husband and children for your support and patience.

Special thanks to…
Governor Jennifer Granholm
Historical contribution: Signed Public Acts 3 2003, House Bill 4079 into law effective April 2003.

Past State Representative Gary Woronchak, (R)-Dearborn
Historical contribution: Sponsoring of House Bill 4079.

Alison Hirschel, Michigan Campaign for Quality Care (MCQC)
Historical contribution: Memberships' six years of continuous efforts (HB 4079)

Jules B. Olsman, Olsman, Mueller & James, P.C.
Historical Contribution: Bryant vs. Oakpointe Villa, Michigan Supreme Court Opinion

…for your support—
Citizens for Better Care (CBC)
National Citizens Coalition of Nursing Home Reform (NCCNHR)
American Association of Retired Persons (AARP)

The Honorable Debbie Stabenow (D)—Michigan, United States Senate
Citizens of the State of Michigan
Citizens of the State of Georgia
Craig Nothnagel and Frank Nowak, UAW Local 22 Retirees
Bishop James I. Clark, Jr.
    Presiding Apostle, Churches of Our Lord Jesus Christ
Bishop William L. Bonner,
    Chief Apostle and Pastor, Solomon's Temple Church, Detroit
Pastor Hollis L. Eason,
    Greater Little Rock Baptist Church, Macon, Georgia
Members of the Churches of Our Lord and Savior Jesus Christ
Dr. Noah Levi, The Southfield Family Dental Center, Southfield, MI
Michael Conners, California Advocates for Nursing Home Reform
Derrick F. Hale, Past District State Representative, Michigan
Family members and friends

> *May God, forever shine His grace and mercy upon each of you.*
> *May God bless the works of your hands.*

Our father appeared as a true leader in the time that the footsteps of a lifetime began...a time of childhood bliss.

Imagining Elizabeth

Elizabeth carefully read the letter repeatedly as she read "California" for the tenth time. She could not believe that her husband was moving their entire family across the country in her present condition. Her fingers played with the envelope and kept patting it on the palm of her hands as she tried to figure out a way to break the news to her mother and father.

Affectionately known as "Big Daddy" and "Big Mama", they were not going to be too happy about this "big" move to another state over a thousand miles away. She could hear her father now, "Liz, I don't like the idea of you going away to California with those five kids and one on the way". He probably would continue by telling her how young she was—"You are young and those kids are young too". Then most of all he would talk about raising the children. "You are going to need some help to train those young ones." Finally, he would express his deepest emotion, as he always have over the years, "Liz, I just have a feeling that I won't ever see you again". He would probably look into her eyes with remorse, yet realizing that it was something his little girl had to do. Elizabeth knew she would have to give them a smile and a kiss to comfort the immediate pain. However, she had her doubts as well. She wondered,

"Could it actually be the last time I would see my parents?"

Family life is full of good times, background, and tragedy. A combination of the three makes up the contents of this book. The good times of childhood, the background of two women's lives, and the tragedy intertwined within both.

From smelling the fragrance of magnolia and dogwood in bloom in southern Georgia, to the sweet smile that crept across Aunt Catherine's face each time she saw me, added the best quality of life to childhood and adulthood.

Yet it is the background, which led the passion to fulfill a quest. Life does indeed come with "background music". Understanding the beat of the music and its origination gives the listener a better reception. The tones, highs, and lows set the rhythm of actions. The tragedy of my aunt's plight in a nursing home fueled the passion to write our story. My chronicling of family trials sets the beat in motion, and introduces the reader to the authoring of a valuable book and resource. Who would have thought that the little red-haired girl born in Savannah, Georgia in 1954 would be the candidate who would ignite a bill of a legislative act in the state of Michigan?

Our mother was beautiful…Ernest loved to
stroke her beautiful hair and call her pretty

Childhood Bliss

✦

Footstep One

The quest of my aunt's plight in a nursing home fueled the passion to write our story. Little did I know that I would represent and then author such a dynamic result. Who would have thought that the red-haired little girl born in Savannah, Georgia in 1954 would tell the twisted and tangled life story? A story of how a family's destiny would evolve into a legislative blessing! Our family life was full of good times; however, we learned all too well that with the good times, bad times linger in the midst. However, this chapter will share childhood bliss. My own life trials will set the stage. Aunt Catherine's story will provide evidence of the sacrifice. The outcome of it all will be a legacy to families near and far.

Despite the fact that our mother was in our lives a very short time, she made an outstanding impression. There were quite a few key decisions she made that would follow her children, their lifetime.

The vivid memory of life began at the tender age of three on the west coast in 1958. We lived in a small framed two-bedroom house with one bath, a living room, dining room, and a kitchen on a military base in Bakersfield, California. Passage through the pathways of my mind, it was as if the small brown terrier, that once bit me on my leg, was still frolicking on the lawn. Our play area was a huge backyard with a wooden table and a swing set that sat on the side of the house. A tall brown wooden fence on one side and a metal fence on the other surrounded our home. The neighborhood was a diverse nation of families. Our immediate neighbors were a multi-racial family who had two little boys who threw rocks over the fence at us quite often. After the frequent volley between the houses, the inevitable happened.

My brother Glenn and I had to visit our neighbors. Along with our mother, we had to apologize for hitting one of the boys in the head with a rock. This was my first encounter with a fast heartbeat and learning to expect the unexpected. The walk next door was the first and last time we made a visit, despite the family continuing to live next door.

Yes, we were a constant adventure. We were "stair-step" children. Just like stairs, we graduated close in age and size. Ernest was the eldest. His seven-year old frame was small for his age. He was cute, with his hair always cut and trimmed in a bowl style, very low on the sides, and his facial features seemed to compliment each other in size and shape. Then there was Glenn. A small round brown-eyed four-year-old who had full lips and a head that appeared too large for his small neck. Glenn was the brainy one. Perhaps that is why his head was so big. I was next (Denise), fair-skinned, red-haired, skinny, and talkative. Then there was Diana, a quiet two year-old who was a bit coy. Michael was our one-year old ebony angel. He was next to the youngest. He stuttered when he talked but easy to get along with, he was the tricky one. Rambunctious and always wanting to play, he seemed to be a happy child. Alonzo, was the youngest, we called him Lonny from the day he came home from the hospital. He rarely cried. By the time my mother was twenty-eight, she had birthed six children.

The neighbors on the opposite side of the "rock throwers" were Caucasian. There were at least ten children with this family. My brother Glenn was the super-hero. He had to fight every morning to get my tricycle back from the youngest boy who was three years of age just as I was. Sometimes Glenn took a good licking, but he always saved my bike from the neighborhood bully, which earned my respect. Glenn, Ernest, and I were a feisty trio. The other two usually followed our lead. Like playing cowboys and Indians, Diana and I were usually participants led by games initiated by my brothers Ernest and Glenn. Well, it turned out that Glenn and Ernest decided that I would be one of the Indians that they would have to tie up and gag in order to rescue the imaginary town. I was always around my mother asking her questions and following her, so it became quite obvious one day that I was nowhere to be found. The boys had placed me behind a sofa and left me. Mamma started calling out to me, but I could not answer. They had tied me up very well. Mamma kept calling and I could only remain silent. The gag was on my mouth very tight. Thank God for mother's intuition. She finally looked behind the sofa, and there I was bound and gagged. Mother called out to the boys to put an end to cowboys and Indians. With her hands on her hips, she sharply warned,

"You could have suffocated Denise boys, don't you ever play like this again."

The boys knew they would need to think of new and creative ways to entertain each other. Cowboys and Indians were the last thing they wanted to discuss right about now.

Ernest would always encourage us to take risks and not to be scary-cats. There was a wooden table in the backyard as I mentioned earlier. One day Ernest asked us to jump off the table into his waiting arms. I had learned from previous challenges the possible results, so I had made up my mind not to volunteer. Everyone took a turn except me. I finally mustered up enough nerve to get upon the table, but jumping was the furthest thing from my mind. Then suddenly I felt a hard pull. Ernest had snatched me off the table yelling,

"Jump scary-cat."

Falling into the grass and receiving a one-inch gash just below my left eye, slightly visible even today, was the reward for my tumble. There was blood everywhere and I started screaming just at its sight. Mamma and Daddy came running. As memory recalls, Dad scooped me up and took me to the hospital on the public bus line. He kept telling me to hold the towel to my face, as onlookers kept staring at us. Arriving at the hospital, the nurses, and staff placed me onto a hard cold table. The doctor kept looking into my face, telling me,

"You'll be alright",

but his words began to slur as I began to get drowsy. The next voice I heard was my father. Daddy was yelling at me to wake up. The doctor picked me up, took me to a mirror, and showed me the bandage on my face. Attempting to hand me over to my dad to hold me, my dad retorted,

"Put her down, she can walk!"

I remember his insensitivity toward my traumatic experience, as if it were yesterday. This remark would become prophesy of my future life with my father. Ernest, needless to say, can still remember the whipping he received when dad and I returned from the hospital. Now mother, she was love all the way; when I came home, she was so genuinely glad to see me. She rocked me and gently kissed my face just below the bandage. She treated the entire incident with the gentleness that only a mother could give.

Mother loved to make sure we laughed before tucking us in for bed. Mother was an attractive, petite woman, with beautiful skin. Her jovial, soft-spoken nature was humble; it was clear though that she possessed a great deal of self-confidence. Even my brothers admired my mother's beauty.

"Mama is one of the prettiest women I know",

Ernest said one day as he rubbed mother's long silky hair. Other family members marveled at the fact about the way that our mother took very good care of herself while carrying us. According to my father, it was complimentary to have other family members recall that mother barely weighed 105 pounds after her sixth child. From all the comments heard about her, she gave me the impression of being very intelligent and very much in love with her family. Our mother affectionately put up with me 'tailing' her throughout the house. Not once would she excuse or send me away.

Breakfast would be ready and waiting for us every morning. By the time we sat down to eat, she would have done morning chores to start the day. The house was spotless, despite ten little feet running through it everyday (and two that were still in the crib). I would remember just staring at my mother, as if I could not get enough of watching her. Not ever, did I see her walk around in nightclothes or her hair undone. Her organization was apparent. She would simply walk to every place in the house and get anything she needed. She stayed busy with us from the time the sun came up in the morning, until the sun set at the close of day. One would think she had only one child, the way we were always clean and dressed. Our disciplinarian, our mother was fair and quick to bring us into correction. One incident makes this fact so clear. I spearheaded a contest with our daily vitamins.

Diana, Michael, and I had taken vitamin pills and licked off all the sugar coating. When we finished as much as we wanted, we threw them into the yard. Our father discovered the pills near the base of the porch steps, where we often sat. The next thing we knew, mother was calling me into the house. How she guessed that it was me, I will never know.

"Denise, did you take those vitamins out of the medicine cabinet?"

Sheepishly, I nodded my confession and she gave me an unforgettable whipping. I learned what a true spanking meant and felt its stinging memory. Our mother did not stop the punishment with the whipping; she also wove a lesson into the whole matter. She explained that my brother, sister, and I could have gotten very sick licking so many vitamins. The lesson stayed with me. I would not ever touch those vitamins again unless our mother gave them to me. Elizabeth, our mother was good to us. From homemade popsicles to the danger of black widow spiders, we learned important things from our mother.

DANGER

There were several memorable incidents in my childhood, which inclined me to record and cherish childhood moments. Record keeping and a good memory was another way I became the storyteller of our lives. There was an incident involving a black widow spider, which etched the meaning of trauma into my young memory. Mother had warned us about playing in the garage. One day our brothers locked Diana and me in one of the caged portions of the garage. Despite the warning from our mother, we decided to play cowboys and Indians with the boys, (and again we were the Indians). When mother found us, she gasped and quickly freed us from our homemade cell. Once out of the garage she called to the boys.

"Ernest and Glenn, it is dangerous in here! Don't you ever do this again those girls could have been bitten by a black widow spider."

We all stood there not knowing what danger really meant, but it had to be something awful from the look in our mother's eyes. She was angry yet relieved that we were all right.

Not long after being captured in the garage, another incident occurred (there were always incidents with six children). I was staring at mother changing Lonny's sheets on the crib; turning my head for a second, mother screamed. Running past me, she told me,

"Watch out", and moved quickly toward the kitchen. She went straight to the drawer and pulled out a large butcher knife. Almost in the same breath, she yelled for my brother Ernest. Fortunately, Ernest was in the backyard near the kitchen door. Mother was moving quickly and frantically, yet able to articulate what she said and did. I asked my mother what was wrong, but she just kept calling for Ernest and grabbed a dishtowel. Standing there, my heart began to pound. The frantic look in her eyes told me something was seriously wrong. Ernest finally arrived through the back door, she handed him the knife.

"Cut me Ernest, right where I am holding this towel."

"No, mama, "wha-no."

"Cut me", she sternly said to Ernest.

Ernest refused. Mother slapped Ernest and yelled,

"Cut me now! I've been bitten by a black widow spider—you must cut me now—I will explain later."

When I heard the words black widow spider, I knew why Mamma's eyes were so wide and afraid. The memory of the scolding to Ernest and Glenn (when we had been locked in the cage) quickly flashed through my memory. While going through my flashback, Ernest had quickly cut Mamma where she directed him on her wrist. I could not remember seeing so much blood gushed as it did from my mother's arm. The blood was more frightening than when cut under my eye. Mother wrapped her wrist with the kitchen towel and quickly ran out the back door. I watched until she was completely out of sight. As she ran, she gave Ernest instructions.

"Get the children in the house and when your Dad gets home tell him about the spider and that I have gone to the hospital."

Ernest nodded with his mouth open. The smell of the exposed blood filtered through my nostrils, I could still smell it to this day.

When our father arrived, we were all watching television. Mother had left early in the day and we did not know how she got to the hospital and not heard from her since she left. Our father looked around and asked,

"Where is your mother?

I beat Ernest to the story of the black widow spider. Dad quickly got us all into the bed, locked the house down, spoke a few words to Ernest, and went out of the door. I knew he was on his way to the hospital.

It seemed as though days had passed before we saw mother again. When we finally did see her, there was a bandage around her wrist and a big smile. She hugged me and then ran to Ernest and hugged him. She told him,

"You were a big boy Ernest and you saved my life."

Ernest beamed from ear to ear. He looked so relieved to see our mother with her arm still on her body. I guess Ernest and mother had more talks about what happened later, but at that moment when he saw Mamma smiling and happy, (with what he had to do)—his look was worth a thousand pictures.

Life returned to the carefree days of childhood. Our mother handled all of our adventures and misadventures. Mother filled our lives with happiness and smiles. She continued keeping the house clean along with the six of us. Yes, our family tree had its share of fruit, bugs, and many lessons.

The woman called Aunt Catherine
pointed out a huge sign on the side of the
mountain that spelled
H-O-L-L-Y-W-O-O-D.

The Road to Aunt Catherine

✦

Footstep Two

The night was dark and full of stars. Amazed at the beauty of God's earth was something my sisters, brothers, and I enjoyed. It was not often that we were able to stay out at night; however, this particular night had a large part of our history woven into its existence. This would be the last night we as a family, would see our mother alive.

We also had visitors that night. Our father had several of his friends over from the military base. Mother had allowed us to stay outside because of his guests. She was very protective of us, yet, respectful of our father's wishes. Allowing us to stay out late that night must have been her compromise for a tough decision.

As the night grew older, it eventually came time for us to go into the house. Mother instructed us all to come in and get ready for bed. Part of getting ready for bed was to make sure that we all used the toilet. When my time came to go to the bathroom, I had an unusual experience. One of the men that had come over to see my father stood at the door while I was using the toilet. Not only did he make me feel uncomfortable, he also just stood there with a scary smile on his face. He was a Caucasian man, and I could tell he had been drinking, he could barely stand. He stood there until I pulled up my underwear. Mother must have seen him leering at me. She yelled out,

"Denise, come out honey and let daddy's guest use the toilet."
With one eye on him and the other glancing at the door mother had given me a way of escape and rescue. The feeling this man gave me caused my skin to feel 'rippled and dirty'. The memory of the feeling etched itself

deeply into my mind, even today. The only thing that kept me from constantly thinking about it was the long talk mother had with us that evening. She must have sensed the tragedy of the night because she took extra time with us as she smiled and said good night.

This night began the long and bumpy road to Aunt Catherine. Along this path were many adults and incidents that lodged themselves in the recesses of my memory. Some of the recollection was pleasant; however, most recalled events were frightening and traumatic. It was unknown for many years that the episodes, which occurred in my life, were incidents of abuse. The conclusion drawn, becoming an adult made it all too clear the gruesome inference of becoming a victim of a heinous crime.

The next day my sister and I woke up in a strange house without my brothers, mother, or my father. It seemed like an eternity before we saw anyone we knew. Despite the friendly faces and kind gestures, Diana and I wondered,

"Where is our mother? Where is our father? What happened to our brothers?"

One day my father came to the gate and brought groceries to the woman with the kind face who apparently had been taking care of us. Looking at our father, Diana and I expected him to take us away. He did not take us away. Instead, he just gave us each a box of licorice candy and told us that he would see us soon. Waving good-bye, we wondered why he had not hugged us or showed any type of sign that he missed us and wanted us to be with him.

Diana cried, it seemed, non-stop. Every day her pillow was wet from tears. Each day, I would find myself rocking her and trying to comfort her. Diana would not eat or talk. The woman with the kind face would ask me to help her get Diana to eat. It was hard not to have our mother, but in my mind I kept wondering where my family had gone. What was even more puzzling was why Diana and I were not with them.

It seemed as if God sent an angel to us ease the pain. The woman with the kind face must have had a son. There was a young handsome man who would come and talk to Diana and I each night. He would tuck us in while giving us a warm smile. Talking with us before bedtime was something that our mother used to do. The loss of our mother had so many twists and turns, to experience a familiar gesture was a treasure.

If ever God sees fit for me to meet the son of the woman with the kind face, I would like to give him the biggest hug! The gentle kindness he gave to my sister and I kept us from feeling so lonely and confused at a very critical time in our lives.

GLENN, GLENN—COME BACK!

One day while Diana and I were playing in the backyard of the woman with the kind face, we briefly saw our brother Glenn. We all, Diana, Glenn, and myself, stood frozen in our steps, locking our eyes onto each other wanting to smile and cry at the same time. Confused, relieved, and excited, it took the strength of Glenn's excitement to break the trance. Glenn quickly gave the woman some money and said,

"Daddy told me to give this to you."

He looked back and stared at me as if he was giving me a mind message and then ran as fast as he could away from the yard. Disappearing down the street, Diana began to cry. No longer was I a pillar of strength—I began to cry as well. The tears flowed for the rest of the evening. It finally dawned on me, it seemed a thousand tears later, that Glenn finally knew where we were and not far away. Yet, the most important part to Diana and I was that we knew it too.

PICKING UP THE PACE DOWN THE ROAD

It was hard for my three-year old little mind to comprehend all of the events that were occurring. However, on another occasion, without any type of notice our father came to the house with my brothers to take us away from the woman with the kind face. Diana and I took off running when were given the permission to go see our brothers. Our father had arrived in a station wagon, so we just knew our mother was somewhere in that big, long, automobile. Diana and I looked around after greeting our brothers, but we did not see our mother. We did however; see a woman sitting where mother should have been sitting. Our father introduced her as Aunt Catherine. Boldly looking into my father's face, I asked,

"Where is mother?"

My father responded,

"Gone away."

At three years of age and happy to be with my brothers and our father, his answer remained sufficient, for the time.

Our father explained to us that he was taking us on a long ride. We were on our way to Macon, Georgia. Leaving California really was a long trip. The woman called Aunt Catherine pointed out a huge sign on the side of a mountain that spelled H-O-L-L-Y-W-O-O-D. She did everything and anything to make us smile. We were not warm to her at all, but she did not give up. Aunt Catherine constantly sang and played with us the best she could on the trip. I remembered her telling Diana,

"Clap your hands, honey,—its fun."

She may have been able to tell that to Diana, but I was not having any part of it. I wanted my mother and she was not my mother, so I did not participate. Ignoring her and attempting to make sure she knew how uninterested I was in all the activities became my goal. The trip from California to Macon was a long ride to pout.

Unfortunately, when we finally arrived in Macon, we (the children), were separated again. Ernest and Glenn lived with our mother's parents, Mr. and Mrs. Floyd Kitchens. Diana, Michael, and I lived with our father's mother, Ella Webb. Our baby brother Lonny moved to Detroit, Michigan with our Aunt Catherine. We did not know where our father lived. Where was our mother? I kept asking myself. After daddy remarried in March 1959 and settled down again, he sent for Lonny from Aunt Catherine in Detroit. The changes and people that came in and out our lives during this time built confusion into our psyche as normalcy. It seemed as if his new wife was our mother, and we thought she was our mother. She wore her hair the same way our mother wore her hair, wore the same type of clothing, and even smiled at us a lot. It was hard to find any differences in the way she looked or the way she took care of us. Deception had begun to make its way early into our lives.

I pretended to use
the bathroom—I did
not like the area
where we had to use
the bathroom.

Puddles in the Road

✦

Footstep Three

Change was common in our lives during this period. Not only were we missing our mother, but we were experiencing physical location changes as well. Having been introduced to several relatives (during our separation in Macon, Georgia), there was one relative that spoiled the experience of "family reunion."

Uncle B. would give me more pennies than he would the other children. He would pull me to his lap and rub my thighs and buttocks. Sometimes he would look down my underwear and touch me in a very personal area. His breath would smell of whisky, but he was never too drunk to look out for other adults nearby. He would continue to touch me and encourage the incidents time after time. He even went as far as making all the other children go outside so he could experience his ill pleasures. The feeling I had for Uncle B. was just like the feeling I experienced with my father's friend looking in on me as I used the bathroom. It was a "creepy" feeling that made me very uncomfortable.

Despite this terrible experience, I still keep in touch with other relatives today who were in this environment. Uncle B. attained his reward. He died because of his whisky drinking. No longer would I have to fear his ever being alone with me again. Like all childhood predators, he told me,

"You better not tell anyone."

As children, instructions were that adults were to 'be respected' and you definitely did not talk back to them. Therefore, Uncle B. kept doing as he pleased to me, with no witness to his guilt.

However, just like puddles in the road on a rainy day, so were the occurrences of life for me as a child. Despite the bad weather and the mess it would leave behind, the sunshine would come and dry up the rain. The flowers bloom and the trees grow. Just like the small peach tree orchard in our grandmother's backyard. Even though she was our stepmother's mother, she did not make us feel any different than if we were her own. She allowed us to have the pick of the peaches when they became ripe. There were so many peaches that my brother Ernest and Uncle Larry would use them (ones that fell off the tree from heaviness) for target practice. Uncle Larry had a 'BB' gun. Ernest was no less daring shooting the 'BB' gun, as he had been most of our life.

Now at the ripe old age of five, Ernest dared me to 'take a shot' from the gun into my foot. You would think I had learned from earlier experiences. He promised it would not hurt. My bold nature took over and I took the challenge and experienced the worst pain ever as the pellet traveled through the shoe into my foot. How could I let myself fall into Ernest's daredevil trap again?

Ernest and Uncle Larry did not stop with the shot in the foot incident—they wanted more excitement. Now they decided to take their gun on the road. Uncle Larry and Ernest decided to shoot down a wasp nest while all the children were playing outside. Well, one could guess what happened. Everyone was stung except those two. Our father whipped them good. Uncle Larry was my father's younger brother. However, they were not finished with their run of adventure yet.

Their next antic really reached beyond 'boyhood' mischief. They were peeping into the bedroom keyhole while mother and father were making love. When they called us (Glenn and I) to look as well, we began giggling and our father heard us. He jumped up and caught us all outside the door. He knew Ernest and Larry put us all up to it. It was evident that the incident made our father very upset. He was so angry that he sent Ernest to Grandfather Floyd's and Larry was not to come over anymore. This incident closed the door to the latest in our life of drama.

GOOD TIMES

The house where we lived with our stepmother and step-grandmother was a two-bedroom house on brick pillars. We were able to play under the house because of how high it would sit off the ground. The bathroom was an enclosed area on the back porch. We would have to use a 'pee pot' during the night. There was no bathtub. Boiled water (from a dipping pail) enabled us to bathe ourselves. This was the same pail used to put water into the wringer washing machine. The wringer washer was the latest technology at the time. I was amazed at how the clothes would go around and around in the big piece of machinery that sat in the kitchen near the doorway. Grandmother would use a stick to help keep the clothes well soaked while she washed. With all of us living there, she washed often. We played in so much red dirt; there was no way to stay clean. Playtime meant dirt time. Dirt was our creative tool. We would make mud pies, mud castles, not to mention throwing dirt at one another. We even used dirt to play make-up, and sometimes we would eat it too. Life in Georgia was very different from life in California.

One major factor in the difference between Georgia and California was Big Daddy. A handsome man about 6'5 with a slender physique and firm hand was the first positive male role model we observed as children. Everyone in the community and in his family knew Big Daddy and his lifestyle. He was a well-respected pillar of the neighborhood. Visitors, who came to his house, knew better than to yell out or holler in his home. There was no smoking, cursing, playing of secular music, dancing, finger popping, or cooking of pork in his house. As a Seven-Day Adventist and Deacon in his church, he took his roles very seriously. Whenever he sat on the porch, even when just passing the house, neighbors made sure to acknowledge him by his last name. He would just nod his head, smile, and give a wave. Big Daddy and Big Mamma (our grandmother) always smiled. Laughing was even better. Each evening, before going to bed, he would have all us cram together in the living room to laugh and talk about the events of the day. He would joke about antics and personality traits in a friendly and loving way. This was an everyday event. If there was important news or broadcasts on the radio during family time, we all had to listen. Television was looked at only when Big Daddy gave the word. The daughters did not wear make-up, pants, or short dresses. Yes, indeed, Big Daddy was the king of his castle. Not only did he provide for his immediate family, but he took care of his grandchildren as well. We lived with Big Daddy and Big Mamma for a short period.

Twelve of us lived in a small three-bedroom house that Big Daddy built. The boys shared a bedroom and the girls shared a bedroom. No one shared Big Daddy and Big Mamma's room. My grandfather told me once that I used to come and get in the bed with him and Big Mamma curling up at the top of his head, making him laugh. Big Daddy showed me so much favor. Their bedroom was in the middle of the house. We could pass through the room from the opposite end of the house; however, we rarely took advantage of the shortcut.

Neither Big Daddy nor Big Mamma tolerated disobedience. Whipping lines meant Big Daddy was chastising everyone. He would go down the line, WHOP, WHOP, WHOP, and WHOP. If you ran or he missed you—that would be two licks for one. One aunt would always run. Big Daddy would always have to catch her before she could take her "lick." Diana and I did not have to get in the line. All we had to do was watch. There was an incident where one aunt received a whipping for wetting the bed. Despite her claim that I had done it, she still got the whipping. I was not about to tell who really had the accident. The days with Big Daddy were some of the good times and memories that I cherish.

TIME TO MOVE

Movement was on the horizon once more. After my father and stepmother moved into a house, we were all reunited. We went back to living as a family in one place with the exception of Ernest, who continued to live with Big Daddy. This was a time I vaguely remembered my aunt, however, I was immediately drawn to her as if we were meant to bond for a lifetime. The bonding feeling became so strong I asked Aunt Catherine, whom I will call "Auntie", whether she could take Diana and I back to Detroit with her—but our father said she could not. Seeing the look in our faces, Auntie asked once more, father did not relent on his decision. The only comfort that she could offer was to come back the next year and try harder to persuade our father to let us go.

SEPTEMBER BLUES

The next year when fall arrived, I was to start pre-Kindergarten (called Reading Readiness) directly across the street from our house. We lived on one of the dirt roads in Macon, Georgia. The only roads that were not dirt roads were the highways. School was a one-room house located on a dirt field with two outhouses as restrooms—one for the girls and the other for the boys. The outhouse was another one of my bad experiences. It was so disgusting; it caused me to learn to hold myself until I got home. If I could not hold myself, I would run across the street and use the house bathroom. Eventually going home—according to the teacher, was unfair to the other children, therefore, it stopped. When the time came to go to the outhouse, I would just stand there looking around, and pretend I used the bathroom. Spiders and bugs were in the outhouse and I had had enough of spiders from the experience with my mother and Ernest having to cut her arm. No, I did not want to have anything whatsoever to do with a spider.

The schoolhouse was so small that it held one large park table with two equal length benches as seats. The chalkboard faced the window and the other walls held elementary posters of the alphabet and pictures. School was frustrating for me as a child because I could not recite my ABCs or count to ten. One little boy tried to help, he would say,

"Repeat after me, 1, 2, 3."

Because I could not remember what came after nine, the tears would begin to flow. Not knowing things on my own caused me to feel helpless. I did not realize that just on the other side of nine was ten. Even the teacher would encourage the other children to help me. I did not enjoy being the focal point. Due to all of the moving and shifting during my fourth and seventh year, the confusion and instability had a lot to do with my short-comings. I did not begin school until just before the age of seven. Not knowing what academically "average" covered; despite my age, I could not attend kindergarten. My stepmother explained how my birthday and all the things going on could affect me this way, and somehow I understood.

Glenn was smart. He was encouraging and told me,

"I could learn."

He would give me chocolate covered wafer candies as a reward for correctly reciting both my numbers and alphabet. That year Auntie did come back to Georgia. After pleading and begging, my father finally gave in, allowed Diana, and I to go to Detroit. The better education pitch sold my dad on the idea. Finally, the old smelly, spider infested outhouse would be a thing of my past. I was so excited to leave, it was a vague memory as to whether or not I even told my parents good-bye. I was glad to be gone for several reasons.

A NEW PLACE...AGAIN

Detroit was definitely a 'new' place. There were no more dirt roads, no mud pies, dirt fields, or outhouses. There was very little dirt as I remembered it. Everything seemed to be full of grass. One of the new rules was that there was to be no playing on the grass. The temptation was great to play on the beautiful green turf and I found myself often challenging the rule, however, I finally adjusted and began to respect and enjoy my new environment.

Auntie enrolled me into kindergarten soon as we arrived. I do not remember the name of the school; I just knew it was big. There were many children. Milk and cookies were our treat just before naptime each day. More exciting than the cookies and milk were the rest rooms. Just as I began to adjust in the new place, Auntie informed us that our father wanted us back home. Therefore, her sister Aunt Thelma took us back to Macon by train.

That summer we returned to Georgia. I did not attend the one-room schoolhouse. Instead, I went to a school similar to the one in Detroit. Despite not going to the dreaded one-room schoolhouse, this was still not Detroit. Writing, reading, and arithmetic no longer made me feel frustrated and I did well academically. Socially, however, I longed for being with Auntie in Detroit. At recess, I did not play with the other children. The teacher would ask me what was wrong. She would ask what she could do to convince me to socialize and play with the other children. An extra cookie was her hook in order to get me to smile. Our normal allowance was one cookie. I knew I just wanted to get back to Detroit.

As time went by, our father starting giving thought to secure a better job and move to Detroit. He often spoke with our stepmother about moving and providing better for his family. Our father Edward did not stay home much. He would leave home often just before the evening set in. We soon discovered that he was regularly going to drink with his friends. With drinking, came all his illusions and perversions.

Glenn, Diana, Michael, and I slept in the same bed in the room with our parents. The girls would sleep at one end and the boys the other. One night, while everyone was asleep, my father awakened me while placing his hand over my mouth. He requested me to remain quiet as he continued to pick me up from the bed. Screaming was my first thought. As I squirmed and attempted to let someone know what he was doing, he would more firmly clasp his hand around my mouth to muffle my complaints. He held his hand there until I calmed down. Everyone was sleep in other areas of the house. Lonny slept with grandmother and Ernest slept on the couch in the hallway.

Eventually, he lifted me toward the floor next to his bed just next to the 'pee pot' and told me not to make a sound. He was obviously drunk. He placed himself on top of me and began to kiss me. I was only seven years old. Attempting to scream my father placed his hand over my mouth before I could get it out. Our stepmother turned facing us asleep; however, she did not awaken. As she moved in the bed, my father began to cover me with his entire body. Peering from under his armpit, I prayed that she would see what was happening. The call was too close, so he returned me to bed. Promising me candy if I did not tell, I placed the entire incident in the back of my mind until the next incident. The next time my father would touch me would be when we moved to Detroit.

BACK TO DETROIT

In 1962, we moved to Detroit. The first location was a small two-bedroom apartment, with Auntie and her husband on Piquette Street on the northeast side of town. There were lots of arguments and too much drinking for an apartment with two families. We were again crowded into a space that was too small for our large family. Diana and I slept on the lower bunk of a bed placed in the dining room. Despite the cramped conditions, the apartment felt huge with no adults there. Playing with each other was usually all we had to do—despite having babysitters who rarely entertained us. When everyone was home, the noise level was very high. I was so happy to see my Aunt Catherine again. We saw Aunt Thelma and Aunt Catherine nearly every day. My father's sisters and brothers would visit as well.

OLD ENOUGH?

The living space cramped our large family lifestyle in the apartment. Our father's relatives visited us often, his drinking continued, as well as advances. We moved into a four-family flat on 12th Street. Now that I was eight years of age, maybe I was old enough and believable. I told my father's youngest sister who immediately told Auntie. Not thinking that their brother could do such a thing to his own child, they took me on a private ride to the store, so I could speak freely. As we rode in the car, I told them what happened. Finally being able to relieve myself of this awful burden, the anticipated solution made my heart beat fast.

Yet, the response my Aunt Catherine gave after I told her what was occurring, was surprising, and disappointing. She said,

"Denise, why would you tell such a lie on your father—he wouldn't do any such a thing as that!"

I felt scolded and ashamed all over again. Was I not only saddened and feeling even more hopeless, a wedge preyed on the relationship between Aunt Catherine and me. It became hard for me to understand why no one could acknowledge and accept what my father was doing. It was sad to learn that adults have trouble understanding perversions too. My father continued to approach me many times after my making the actions known—I was trapped—who would I tell? There was no longer a desire to risk losing the love of my family to tell them something they did not believe was happening. They never believed it was happening. The greatest fear was that they would consider me a liar if father's side of the story would be more convincing.

Our father took his warped sexual appetite to a new level. One day when all the adults were away, he once forced my brother Glenn and I into the bathroom. Glenn and I had always been friends and talked a lot to one another. Apparently, our father was jealous of the relationship. He sneered at us and said,

"Since you two are so close and can't stand to be apart, don't you come out of that bathroom until you "do it" to each other."

He then pushed us into the bathroom and stood with the door slightly ajar instructing Glenn to kiss me on the mouth since he loved me so much. Glenn and I would look at each other with the same surprised glances that we experienced when we saw each other after our mother's sudden disappearance. In an angry tone, he shouted,

"Kiss her I said!"

Glenn, not knowing what he might do to either of us, reluctantly kissed me on the lips. Our father shut and locked the bathroom door, instructing us not to come out until we engaged in sex. It seemed like an eternity before he came back. As we heard him beginning to unlock the door, we positioned ourselves close together as if we had followed his ill and sick command. After opening the door, he asked us whether we had done what he said. We both nodded affirmatively. He let us out and warned us that we should stop playing with one another and being so close because boys should play with boys and girls should play with girls. Glenn and I never told or shared with anyone what had happened. We only discussed it once as adults.

LASALLE BOULEVARD

The road then moved us into one of the most beautiful houses I had ever seen. We moved onto a street called LaSalle Boulevard. The house was brick with four bedrooms located on Detroit's west side. The house was located in a nice upscale area. All of the houses were huge and the lawns well manicured. The streets, lined with full, healthy trees, looked as if someone had placed them neatly in a row. Our house was a corner lot with a three-car garage. The backyard was in full bloom with brightly colored flowers. There was a path leading to the garage lined with flowers as well. A path of luscious green vines had begun to weave itself in and out of the holes of the white wooden overhead fenced arch.

The inside of the house was just as beautiful. There were fireplaces in the living room and the master bedroom. The oversized kitchen boasted of a dishwasher, a breakfast nook, and a dual opening that led to the formal dining room. The kitchen also had a door that led to one of the most beautiful and roomiest basements. The basement had a one-half bath, a laundry room, a utility room, and a wet bar. We enjoyed playing in the basement. Because of our father's liquor, we (the children) did not go down into the basement without an adult. Another pleasant surprise was that soon after we settled in, Aunt Catherine and her husband moved into the house.

We dressed in our stoles
for the LaSalle house
parties...these were good
days—

Joy in the Fire

✦

Footstep Four

Auntie and her husband coming to live with us on LaSalle seemed to be one of our father's better decisions. It seemed as if the house was now full of happiness and freedom. Nothing we did seemed to bother her. She would play with us often. To keep us entertained, she taught us games that burned our energy. There were games like Rock Teacher, where we had to start at the bottom of the stairs and advance by guessing which hand she held a rock. We also learned how to play table games like Chinese and regular checkers. There were too many board games to name. She taught us string games like 'cup in the saucer', pencil games like Hangman and Squares. She even allowed us to experiment with our vocal chords by teaching us nursery rhymes and sing-a-longs. The most fun for me personally was when she taught me how to ride a two-wheeled bicycle.

Foot racing was another event that she would challenge with us. Auntie was so fast; she would always give me a head start. I did not realize how much fun running would become. Running became a very favorite sport of mine. By the time I reached fourth grade, I was on the school's track team. My first track meet was at the convention center in an All-City Track and Field event. As I looked around, the arena was big and intimidating as well as the competition. Track became my sport of choice until the 10th grade. With Auntie's inspiration and faith in me, I even participated in the running broad jump in a city competition and track meet for my age group, placing third in the 220. Yes, Auntie was indeed, the joy in the fire. The joy was all that she taught me as well as living in such a beautiful home. One Christmas, while living on LaSalle, Diana and I were given a faux mink stole and a very big doll house from Auntie. During Christmas, father would come into the house with the largest live Christmas tree I ever saw. He had to trim the top to keep it from touching the ceiling. We could hardly wait until Christmas morning to see our gifts. One early Christmas morning, some of us crept downstairs and saw Mamma, our father, and Auntie placing presents under the tree and became shocked to find out they were Santa. Each Christmas, while living on LaSalle, we received many presents. Tuesday was daddy's payday; he would bring home sugar canes, fresh coconut and pineapple. The joy of sucking on the sugar canes and cracking the coconuts were what I remembered the most.

Auntie taught me so many constructive things to do with myself. On the other hand, my father continued to take advantage of his incredulous urge to abuse me. The fire was all the pain and ugliness that went on in this beautiful house. My father and stepmother, who we now were calling 'Mamma', were having regular basement parties. Mamma would dress up as if she was going to a local night club, wearing her favorite tight fitting little red dress and shoulders draped with a mink stole Father gave her one Christmas. Her tiny waist accented her shapely hips. She would often ask all of us what should she wear. We knew Mamma wanted to wear that red dress and we wanted to see her in it. Obviously, our response was always a consensus, "the red dress Mamma". Then we would ask her to play the record with the lyrics, "Put on your red dress baby, and dance with me tonight". Mamma would spin around, shake her hips and we would all break out into a laugh.

With those basement parties came liquor, relatives who like to party, and unknown to my parents, other child predators who liked little girls. Now, not only was my father having his way with me, so were others. One other male relative was trapping me and forcing his affections on me as well. There was no safe haven in the house and the intimidation not to tell loomed over me like a heavy metal blanket. What was even more ironic was that my father did not know what the other relative was doing. Whenever Mamma or Auntie left the house, I would ask to go with them. The most memorable incident was when my greatest fear became reality. On one of the occasions when they went to the store, the intuition of what was to befall me happened. As Mamma and Auntie were leaving, I begged to go with them. They instructed me to stay home with the other children and they would be back shortly. I tugged and pulled until Mamma turned to me and said,

"No Denise, stay here, I said we would be right back."

My father had been drinking and I began to tremble. Shaking and walking fast, I followed Mamma and Auntie down the street. Once they spotted me, they immediately instructed me once again to go home. Reluctantly I stood there on the sidewalk. The front door was still visible from where I stood. Obediently turning around and taking steps (as slow as I could), back toward the house, was all I could do. Eventually, my gut feeling did not fail me. Father was standing at the door, as if he knew my plan. He instructed me to come into the house and told the other children to go outside to play. At nine years of age, all the trapped feelings of a caged animal dropped into my mind. Again, I shut out the horror and tolerated another session of molestation.

My step-grandmother came to visit one summer during our stay on LaSalle and I begged to go back to Georgia with her. She and mamma discussed it and I was allowed to go with her. We traveled by car and I remember vomiting nearly the whole ride due to motion sickness. After arriving in Georgia, I stayed the summer with my father's mother—Big Mamma Ella. It was the best summer ever. Big Mama was so kind and she gave me freedom to be a child. She took me to church regularly and also taught me to pray nightly before going to bed. This teaching came in handy the following years. Whenever I was hurting, sad, or faced with an awful situation, I prayed to God for help.

Father's lifestyle and 'woman on the side' saw to it that our lifestyle changed. Eventually, the house on LaSalle Boulevard went into foreclosure. We went from glamour to gloom—everything gradually changed. We packed up our toys and clothes, and all the dreams that could have been. It was as if everything that had brought us joy went 'poof' like a magic spell. Yet, there were things that I did not miss. I did not miss the hiding and running. I did not miss the parties or the company. Life has a

way of combating the worst fears in the most amazing ways. Leaving
LaSalle Boulevard was salvation for my youth that had been under attack.
Only until after I became an adult could I mention the horrible events of
LaSalle Boulevard to Mamma. She wept when I told her why I begged her
to take me with her every time she left the house. There was little comfort
for her tears.

We went so far down the economic ladder; there would be no place to
go except up. In 1965, we moved into a four-bedroom upper flat in
Detroit's Black Bottom district. Infested with roaches and creaking floors,
we watched Mamma wash in a bathroom. The conditions were so deplor-
able; it took imagination to escape the reality. Ernest, the eldest boy, kept
running away from home, he was so angry and disappointed. Fighting
with other children became my way of resenting the living conditions to
which we had succumbed. School became a safe haven. The nurturing
environment of home had gradually deteriorated, only replaced with the
public school system. The open expression of my thoughts and dreams
suffocated in the small living area. In school, it seemed as if my ideas and
dreams would gain new life. *It all became a focus of walking in what I knew
I could become instead of what I could see.* Learning how to exercise faith in
dire circumstances brought out the leader in me. At school, I could be
whoever, and do whatever I wanted. Intelligence, creativity, and show-
manship came full circle during school. It was important to have an
opportunity to feel what being "top" meant. Authorities and peers began
to respect my choices.

In one example, a teacher who did not tolerate talking or disobedience
in his classroom, gave me my first platform. The male instructor had told
the class to stop talking. He accused me of continuing to talk after his
instruction. Despite telling him that I was not talking, he continued the
'consequence's of disobedience. Apparently, during this time corporal
punishment existed in public schools.

He called me to the front of the classroom. The next instruction was to
turn my backside to the class and bend over. The request alone was humil-
iating. After hitting me once, I straightened myself, looked him into the
eye, and told him not to hit me again. He raised his voice and instructed

me back into the bent over position. Remaining erect, I walked toward the door. Sternly retorting,

"Denise, get back here!"

I confidently responded,

"No."

Then I took exit not only from his room, but also out of the door of the school. The echo of gasps as I walked through the room rested in my ears all night. He had run to the door of the classroom giving me further instruction. He told me not to come back unless a parent was with me.

The next day Mamma did accompany me to school. We had a meeting with an opportunity to give my side of the story. Not only did I express my dissatisfaction with the method by which he chose to discipline me, I also shared my conclusion. With the utmost sincerity, I told them both,

"If this happens to me again, I will do it all over again. Furthermore, I may hit the teacher back too."

I could feel the solid sureness of my words as they left my mouth. Naturally, my comments made it to the teacher's lounge, because no other teacher ever attempted to chastise me in that manner any more. However, the incident did not stop it from happening to other students.

Despite the paddling incident, school was peace, which allowed me to express my creativity and competitive spirit. I joined nearly every after-school program available to me, including Saturday morning creative writing classes. Life became tolerable. Mamma often came to the school looking for me when I failed to return home timely, after school.

Later I became witness to an incident where a student, paddled on her knuckles, began to bleed. Knowing how she felt, (and probably worse), I suggested that she leave and go tell her mother. The act brought about such a commotion, that it ended in me throwing down my 'honor earned' safety belt. This was my first realization that I recognized a *fighting spirit*. Not only did I want to fight for my own freedoms, but also it felt right to fight for someone else to benefit from the trail I had blazed.

Abuse had given me a different slant on viewing adults and their powerful position. Despite the courage, fighting for what was right; I personally would not be able to find this strength at home for myself until later in life.

We would ask

Mamma often who was

the woman in the picture.

She would respond with,

"Someone who

loved you very much."

MRS. ELIZABETH FORD

The remains of Mrs. Elizabeth Ford who died in Mojave, Calif. a few days ago, arrived in Macon Monday afternoon. Funeral services for Mrs. Ford will be held today at 3 p.m. at the Seventh Day Adventist Church on Spring St. Burial will be at Woodlawn Memorial Park. Mrs. Ford is survived by her husband Sgt. Edward Ford, six children, Ernest, Glenn, Denise, Diane, Michael, and Alonzo Ford; her mother; three brothers; three sisters; a mother-in-law. Mrs. Ella Ford Eason of 856 Lexington St. The funeral cortege will leave from 1352 Ft. Hill St.

Breaking Down Walls

✦

Footstep Five

In order to relieve the stress of home life, the outings at school become necessary. The sensation of winning 'spelling bee's at the classroom level alone was just enough to keep me focused. Nevertheless, it is when I discovered poetry that I really gained momentum. A poem I had written appeared in the school's newsletter, this event really heightened my goal setting. If there was a function at school, I was trying to join it. It did not discourage my efforts even when I applied for band and not accepted (because I could not sing the do-re-mi chord). School kept me from being at home. Not only were the clubs interesting and psychologically rewarding, my social skills had developed. The distance from home to school was about a mile and a half. Mamma would scold me about me being late from staying after school and joining so many clubs. However, I realized that scolding me was merely an expression of her concern for my well-being.

Auntie did not visit us much while we lived in that four-bedroom upper flat. Apparently, when we moved Auntie had secured a separate dwelling. She worked for a doctor in the suburbs of Detroit. The doctor had children who were probably a little older than we were. She would bring us clothes, toys, and even bikes they had outgrown. Auntie knew we missed having nice things and like always, she wanted to make it better for us. Ten-speed bikes were the style when we were growing up. We had two big bikes called a 'truck bike.' Unlike a ten-speed, it was not stylish it was awkward. Just the sensation of taking turns and having something to ride made us happy. Despite their awkwardness, those bikes were our pride and joy. Other children had to worry about laying their bike in the wrong place or having their bike stolen, however, we did not. When other children's bikes were not working or stolen, we were one of the few families still riding because no one wanted a 'truck bike.' We rode those bikes proudly for two years. Glenn, Michael, and Lonny often portrayed Batman, Robin, and the Joker or Green Hornet. They would use the bikes to ride to their Bat Cave, which consisted of a high mound of dirt nearly hidden by trees in a downtown development zone. Michael played the villain switching between the Joker and Green Hornet. They would ride the bikes without any shame dressed like each character. There were certain days they played their favorite characters and Diana and I knew there was no sharing of the bikes on those days. The boys seemed to want more attention from our father. I believe their near daily portrayal of these make-believe Gotham City characters was a mental escape from the life they actually lived to a life of make-believe. They were playing the "hero "to people who needed help from those who misused and abused them. Perhaps the characters they portrayed spoke to their own wish for a victor to the villain.

Even though Auntie did not visit often, we did spend time with our Aunt Thelma nearly every other weekend. Sometimes Diana and I would spend the weekend with Auntie and earn money. Aunt Thelma taught us cleanliness, grooming, and behavior. Auntie taught us thriftiness. She taught us how to do things with our hands, and most importantly, how to earn a dollar. Diana and I would clean and iron at a neighbor's house and paid $2.40 for a half days work, from 8:30am to 1:00pm on Saturdays. We shared the proceeds with each other. The work ethics and practice came from within our family in many different ways.

WALLS BEGINNING TO FORM

Even while we were living in these disgusting conditions, our father did not "wake up" to the damage he was causing his family. His drinking again became regular, as did his approaches toward me. He began to make the occasions more frequent than before. I had to escape mentally to an even higher dimension of thought to escape the knowledge and awareness of what he was doing to me. It was hard to believe that Mamma knew nothing about his advances, but it was clear that she did not. Breaking down the walls of hatred took me into another dimension.

There had to be some relief from the pressure that was entering my life. I had to believe there was a higher purpose for me going through this gross trespass of my rights as a human being. The road to escape was still far off. However, I had to believe, just believe, there was a rescue coming.

Fear was an everyday occurrence while living in 'Black Bottom' (known as the first black regiment in Detroit and near the downtown area). The sirens and sounds of the drunks that "hung out" at the alley corner hummed in my mind. Derelicts sitting in front of abandoned houses in chairs and old car seats, as if it were a proper homestead, were common. Seeing a woman stabbed in the head during an apparent attack was not something the average child would want to witness. These were the types of the many bloody squabbles witnessed in our neighborhood. Between the fights at the high school, constant "break-ins" at the corner grocery store, and burglars regularly looming outside our bedroom window; it was hard to concentrate on a normal life. Drama was an understatement related to the exposure we experienced in Detroit's Black Bottom.

There was no genuine respect for the police—it was fear, yet it kept peaceful residents on guard. The police force, which patrolled our neighborhood, were called the 'Big Four.' They were nicknamed as such from their structure. The 'Big Four' consisted of four white male police officers who rode in unmarked police cars. Black-on-black crime was prevalent, so the only perpetrators were black and law enforcement was white—racial tension was high. Even Mamma's opinion was that this team enjoyed arresting and beating black people in the streets of Detroit with their legal freedom.

WALL OF CURIOSITY

It was in this small cramped place that my siblings and I began to pay more attention to the woman in the photo, on top the television. We would ask Mamma often who was the woman. She would respond with,

"Someone who loved you very much."

Mamma would never tell us her name or what connection she had to us. We would ask her so many questions about the photo until one day she gathered us all together and told us it was our birth mother. Since I was only three when my mother died, I did not believe her. Mamma had been the only woman I recognized as a child, despite spending time with my actual mother. Now it was clear why my father made sure he married someone that looked and acted like our mother. I asked her,

"Then who are you if (pointing to the picture) she is our mother? What happened to her? Why are you here instead of her?"

My questions ran together it seemed, all in one breath. Mamma went on to explain that she was actually our stepmother. She told us our real mother had died and went to heaven. Of course, at the age of curiosity, we all wanted to know the answers to the same questions, like,

"How did she die?"

Mamma told us it was not her place to tell us and tiredly sighed saying,

"I have probably told you too much already."

She closed the discussion with a suggestion that we ask our father for more information. For once, we could hardly wait for him to come home, to ask about our mother.

The look on his face was clear that he was upset about our questions. He was not only upset, he was outright mad. He snapped back that he would tell us when he felt we were ready. Well with me being 10, Ernest 15, Glenn 11, Diana 9, Michael 8, and Lonny 7, we felt indeed ready. Realizing that he was not going to discuss the photo or talk to us about it, we decided to hold our questions. Even though my sister and brothers seemed to settle for his answer, I did not. My source would be Auntie.

Waiting to see Auntie seemed like an eternity. She would be the ideal person to ask her about my mother. Just knowing that she was fair and cared about us, seemed likely that the information would just roll from her mouth and we would know the truth. To our surprise, Auntie would not tell us how our mother died. She must have read off the same script as Mamma. The woman that we could share secrets with and tell all our dark, deep, thoughts could not tell us about our mother. It was now clear that Mamma and Auntie were good friends. I did not know just how close they were until Auntie held this information back from us.

We went back to our father with another appeal. This time he became more firm and stubborn.

"I will tell you when I am ready and not before—don't ask me about this anymore", would be his reply to the many requests.

During one of his episodes where he approached me, he kept telling me how much like my mother I resembled. He would talk of her beauty and being pretty. The act he committed toward me would become more confusing than ever. Did he hate her? Did he not know that what he was doing to me was not love or admiration? The intensity of what my father was doing to me had begun to invade my intellect. How I wanted to tell Auntie, but the memory of the first time I told her was all too clear. Instead, I chose to enjoy the times with her that I could and push the incidents and ugliness aside. Breaking down walls of resentment and pain was all I seemed to do in these troublesome times. There had to be a better way!

The rats were
soooo big!

Predators Galore

✦

Footstep Six

There were predators galore during this stage of my life. When was it ever going to stop? The desire to stay away from home grew more appealing every day. After joining the city's recreational track and softball teams, it seemed the situation at home would only get worse. Continuing as my father's sex toy was bad enough. Yet, it seemed like there was an invisible conspiracy to drive me out of my mind—another predator had entered my life. A different uncle had begun to fondle my breast at every opportunity. He would give me money not to say anything about it. Yes, every chance to stay away from home was a welcome rescue. I even began spending nearly every weekend with Auntie or Aunt Thelma just to get relief. The aggression and anger I felt began to grow inside of me like a disease. It would manifest itself through fighting with other children, mostly bullies in the neighborhood. It did not matter to me whether it was a peer or adult, gang member, male or female, big or small. I felt it my personal obligation to challenge them all. Fighting continued up to my senior year in high school. I would even challenge teachers who exhibited a disregard for young people.

NEW INVADERS

Predators would manifest in all shapes, ways, and forms. The next new invaders were in the animal form, which took the third ring of my already two-ring circus. The rats that took over at night in the four-bedroom house on Fisher Street, after the move from Black Bottom, became the next invaders. The bedroom Diana and I shared was near the top of the stairs. This would be the first room the rats entered. We were so afraid at night we would sleep with sticks, hugged up together, and with the covers pulled over our heads. Often we would lay awake listening to see if the rats would get on the bed. Our eyelids would get so heavy we would fall asleep from trying to stay awake. Each night brought its own challenge. Since we had gotten use to the patter of rat's feet running up and down the stairs, it would not awaken us right away. Only when they became louder (which would mean more rats than usual) would we awake. After awakening, we would be wide-awake. We then would step upon our dresser from the bed to turn on the light. One night after entering our bedroom, I thought one had gotten on the bed. Shaking the covers and quickly stepping onto the dresser to turn on the light became a skill. They moved so quick, it was hard to catch them in the act.

A clothing rack was our closet. We could see the rat hanging within the clothes on the rack. That was our first glimpse of his incredibly long tail. The tail on this rat had to be 12 inches long and fat. We did not even want to see the rat if his tail was that big. Our imagination did a good enough job to convince us to keep the light on. The rat did not move and neither did we. Diana and I could not remember when we fell asleep. Staying with Auntie or Aunt Thelma was a welcomed exodus from the rats. Despite these embarrassing conditions, Mamma and our father still entertained lots of company regularly. Guests did not to stay all through the night as they did when we lived on LaSalle.

Revelation and knowledge met us at every angle. One summer our birth mother's youngest sister moved to Detroit to be with her husband. I had met her when we lived with Big Daddy in Macon. She was the aunt who was responsible for bathing and clothing Diana and me. While in Detroit, she would occasionally take Diana and I to her apartment to spend the night. One day, as she was preparing to take us back home we asked her about our mother's death. We had also asked that she not tell that we had questioned her about it. The inquiry had to be a secret. Attempting to make it clear that it was something she was not to tell, she finally relented and told us that someone who loved us very much had killed her. She needed to say no more—Diana and I looked at each other. In awe, we asked whether it was our father. She replied in a soft whisper,

"Yes."

She also mentioned how she would probably get into trouble for telling. We then asked why the incident had been kept from us for so long. She responded,

"Your daddy was afraid you kids would stop loving him."

We looked at her like—what a joke! Anger drove me to wanting to know more about the whole incident. We wanted to know more details. We asked,

"How did she die?"

She responded,

"Your father shot your mother."

Her answer caused Diana and I to nearly buckle at the knees. She closed the conversation at this point and asked us not share what she had revealed to us about what happened. I was so 'hot' with anger, as soon as we arrived home; I wasted no time in asking my father why he shot my mother? There were other relatives in the house at the time of my pointed question. Diana and I quickly informed our brothers of what we had learned about our mother's death. Mamma became quiet and our father asked us,

"Who told you your mother had been shot?"

We looked over toward my mother's sister and pointed. Our father looked quickly toward his sister-in-law and began yelling at her,

"I will tell them when I am ready and not before. It was not your place to tell them."

All of the other adults looked at my aunt as if she had just committed the greatest act of betrayal. We were immediately, sent to our room as the adults began to argue with one another. It was clear that they were targeting their opinions and anger toward my mother's sister.

Later on, we learned that my father had asked her to leave and never come back into his house again. My mother's sister left Detroit soon after and returned to Georgia. Diana and I felt sad to see her leave and especially after exposing her as the one who told us about the shooting. When we apologized to her, she smiled and told us she was not upset with us. She said that someone should have told us long before now. She felt we needed to know what had happened. She also told us that she was relieved we knew and the big secret was over.

Our curiosity did not stop at this incident. We wanted to know that all-important question. Was it intentional or accidental? The only two who would know that truth would be our biological mother and father. He was not telling and mother was not alive and could not tell. The only closure that would come of the incident would be after I had grown up as an adult. Revelation came once again through a car trip with my grandfather, Big Daddy. One year while visiting him, he told me to get into my car and take him somewhere. When 'Big Daddy' gave you an instruction, you just did it—one did not ask questions. As we got into the car, 'Big Daddy' gave all the directions. I did not even think about asking him where we were going, I trusted Big Daddy. He directed me onto a highway not far from his house and instructed me to make a series of right turns. The right turns led down a dirt road and into a cemetery. When we arrived at the spot in which he wanted me to stop the car, he said,

"Stop right here and get out of the car."

I did exactly as he told me. He continued as he pointed,

"This is where your Mamma is buried and don't tell anyone I took you here." He stood there with me as I watched in surprise and then slowly he walked back to the car. As I knelt down toward the grave, I began to wipe the dirt off her headstone—it read 'ELISABETH FORD'. After reading her name, it made me angry that someone had misspelled her name. Immediately, being the rectifier that I had grown to become, I thought about getting the name corrected, and said my goodbyes to join my grandfather. After returning to the car, I looked into my grandfather's eyes and told him,

"Thank you."

He looked back into my eyes and responded,

"You're welcome—now take me to the store."

I think the purpose of visiting the store was to account for the time we had been gone. Big Daddy wanted no questions upon our return.

Years after that visit, I often thought about making the correction to the headstone, but thought to leave well enough alone. You see, I never learned whether that was actually how she spelled her name. I believe that 'Big Mamma' would have known how to spell her own daughter's name. However, I did learn that mother spelled her name with a "z" instead of an "s" but it just did not matter anymore. When I became a grandmother myself, I requested that my daughter spell her daughter's middle name ELISABETH as written on my mother's headstone. It seemed to give me closure and a voice of statement for what happened to her.

Big Daddy and I would share many other private moments together before and after the visit to mother's gravesite. He would tell me things about life, primarily his and his relationship with the Lord. He would remind me so often that no matter where I go in life or who I become, live righteous, and drink plenty of water to ensure long life. Big Daddy took his leave just after his 105th birthday, March 23, 1985. A short time after hospitalization for the first time in his life, his eyes closed, in sweet rest. "Big Daddy" did not like hospitals and used herbs for all his ailments. Oftentimes I believe that the act of hospitalization may have ushered his life into rest. Missing Big Daddy is part of my life, because he was my model of a "good man." Big Mamma, so very special and sweet took her rest (several years later) shortly after honoring her at our first family reunion. She died November 23, 1992. The pound cakes she would bake on my travels from Georgia to Detroit were so good one could taste the memory. Her biscuits were tastier than any commercial or other home-made biscuits. With both grandfather and grandmother gone, I seldom make as many visits to Georgia—it is just not the same any more, despite the other relatives that live there whom I love very much.

In my innocence, father's behavior went unrecognized and incomprehensible to me. His punishments severe and his total disrespect taught me to hate him—yes, my father taught me real anger.

Series of Pain

♦

Footstep Seven

Once my mother's sister returned to Georgia, things quieted down around the house. Diana and I continued to spend the weekends with Auntie and Aunt Thelma. There was an occasion when we had gone visiting at a neighbor's house while at Aunt Thelma's. Our father had come to get us. Returning home after getting the message that our father was there to pick us up, our father, three of our uncles, and a couple of Aunt Thelma's neighbors were in the living room. It was clear that the men had been drinking. Being in what seemed to be a "safe zone" took me a bit off guard, so Diana and I went into the kitchen to get a glass of water. Aunt Thelma was in the kitchen. Father angrily entered the kitchen, scolding us for not knowing where we were. After drinking the water, we began to walk out of the kitchen. With a slight shove, father told Diana to hurry, but then he turned toward me and grabbed my collar. He swung his hand back and slapped me across the face so hard that my head hit the refrigerator and my nose began to bleed. Apparently, he thought I had snickered or made some type of gesture when he shoved Diana.

"Take that smirk off of your face, nothing's funny", he bellowed into my face. The pungent smell of the alcohol spewed as he spoke. I had no idea what he was talking about and stood there baffled. This had been the second time father hit me and caused my nose to bleed. In a brief moment of strength, I felt the desire to fight back. Pacing the floor in confusion and anger, not knowing what to do, I just stood there and stared. Looking into his face, I could only see his anger and hate. His eyes seemed to penetrate my soul, as if I was the catalyst to his doom. It was as if I held his future and he did not know how to get it out of me except by hitting or beating it out of me. Confused and angry as to how could my own father stare at me with such hate and venom in his eyes. I began walking out of the kitchen into the living room. Looking around for my coat hastily from one side of the room to the other, I just wanted to leave and run away. My father followed me, yelling another threat,

"Ya wanna do something, huh? Do something if you want and if you look at me again like that, I'll bust you upside your head with this ash tray,"

he grunted out with a dark harsh tone. As he reached and picked up a heavy thick glass ashtray, I believed he would have made his threat good. Not one adult said a word to him. I looked pleadingly at them, hoping that someone would come to my rescue. Diana who was standing nearby silently moved closer to me. It was as if she would be ready to defend me if no one else would. Father gave her a threatening glaring stare as she turned away. She would look back at me briefly, signaling as to what she was doing. Finally, Aunt Thelma told father to put the ashtray down and let her take care of my bloody nose. He calmed down a bit and lowered the ashtray. He then allowed Aunt Thelma and me to leave the room. After returning from the bathroom, Father told us to get into the car—he was taking us home. Diana and I sat quietly, not even speaking to one another, during the ride home. Once arriving at the house, the car barely came to a complete stop, I jumped out of the vehicle crying. Running into the house and dashing into my parent's bedroom. Father kept his shotgun over the bed. I practically knocked Mamma over jumping over her onto the bed to grab the gun. Mamma quickly grabbed me and the gun, wanting to know what was wrong. All I could do was frantically tell her, "I am going to kill him." She questioned,

"Who, who are you going to kill—what is going on?", as she secured the rifle from my hand.

I screamed back to her,

"Father—he hit me again for no reason and made my nose bleed."

Mamma said calmly,

"Your father has slapped me before, but I haven't taken the gun to him." Shocked by her calm manner and hearing that she too had been hit did not quench the fire my father started at Aunt Thelma's. Undaunted, I said,

"Well, I am going to kill him for the both of us!"

By this time, father was coming up the stairs. Mamma told me to leave the room. Not wanting to let it go, I stood there telling Mamma that he had no right to hit me. Father entering the room said,

"I'll do it again." I responded in a cold and smooth voice—"If you do, I *will* shoot and kill you", then left the bedroom to go to my bedroom. Diana was waiting. I shut the door. Diana and I hugged each other in comfort as we had done so many times before.

The next day father apologized and offered to allow me to slap him back insisting that I do it. He literally took my hand; raising it to his face. Naturally, he had been drinking again. Responding to his offer with a quick,

"No", and immediately leaving his presence, I ran from the house to the neighborhood playground.

It began to sprinkle as Diana ran behind me. Finally, reaching the playground, I stopped and looked up.

"Denise, Denise, what are you doing?—why you keep looking up into the rain that way…what's the matter?" my sister called to me as I spun around in the rain.

Hoping that the rain would wash all the icky feeling off, I kept spinning. It was as if God was giving me my own personal shower right in front of everyone to show everyone that He loved me. Feeling clean was something I liked and still do today.

In my innocence, father's behavior went unrecognized and incomprehensible to me. His punishments severe and his total disrespect taught me to hate him—yes, my father taught me real anger.

"I'm getting cleaned Diana, cleaned by the rain", answering as if it was an official announcement.

Playing on the swings and tilting her head from side to side, my sister just stared at me as if I just came from another planet.

"Denise", she said, "Let's go home."
Before going to sleep that night, I fell to my knees asking God to help me. I knew he had heard me. I felt a warm feeling come all over me, as if God was assuring me that everything would be all right. The tears that had filled my face so many times helped me find relief. It was the prayerful relief of coming to the Lord with my problem. It was my hope that prayer would stop father's treatment of me and stop the incidents.

The feeling of relief was short lived. Only a few days had gone by when father arrived home very late one evening. It was apparent he had been drinking again. His obvious heavy footsteps were always an indicator as he came up the stairs. Mamma, soundly asleep, was in the bed. She had been drinking with friends that day. Diana and I looking at each other in fear, moved closer to one another in the bed. Mamma and father's room was next to ours. We clinched each other tighter as we heard father bumping around in his bedroom. Fear became reality when father called out my name. I intentionally did not answer, to make him think I was asleep. He called out to me again saying,

"I know you hear me calling you, you are not asleep" (as if he could read my thoughts).

I groggily answered. He told me to go get him a glass of water from the kitchen. I asked Diana to go with me but she was afraid because of the rats that so often had their run of the house after dark.

Upon returning to his bedroom with the glass of water, father asked me to go into the bedroom that was next to his and wait on him. Before I could leave the room, Mamma sat up in the bed angrily, turning toward me,

"Don't you go anywhere but to your room and get into bed."
She quickly turned her face toward father, telling him in an equally angry tone,

"You thought I was sleep—how dare you molest your own daughter."
She began yelling at him, letting out all that she had suspected come into the open.

"I knew you were doing something, I just couldn't put my hands on it. You no-good bastard—screwing your own daughter."

She spilled the words out in the air and they rang through the house. She must have mustered the courage from her drinking that afternoon—she let it all out! Father began to act as if Mamma did not know what she was saying. He knew she had been drinking and tried to take advantage of the fact. Mamma shut the door and continued yelling at father. Diana and I became even more afraid. We did not know what was going to happen next. My heart pounded rapidly—thinking Mamma would be angry with me. We picked up a baseball bat that was next to my bed. We laid it between us should we need to defend ourselves. Both of them were violent and loud. Diana always slept with a butter knife. She had placed it in her hand, ready to strike at any moment. Our bodies shook against each other in fear as we huddled and prayed. After an hour or so of arguing, Mamma, and father, quieted down and apparently fell asleep. Once we realized that neither of them were entering our room and hearing the loud snores, Diana and I felt it safe to go to sleep ourselves, and we did, in each other's arms.

The next morning Mamma was silent around the house. Mamma exposing him caused my father to stop the sexual molestation for a while. The next time this subject would come from Mamma's lips was for clarity after the next grueling episode in my life.

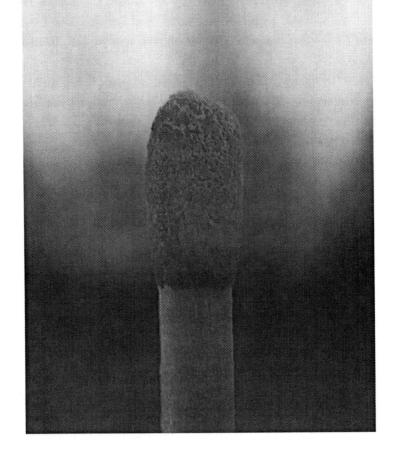

"The moon was full and lit the area where he had parked. I knew at this point, he had taken me to a place where he knew no one would hear my cries or screams."

External Predator

✦

Footstep Eight

Staying away from home had its down side to life as well. At 15, I had secured a summer job washing dishes at a downtown restaurant on Woodward. My work hours were from six until ten at night. My father was to pick me up from work, however, something happened and Mamma had asked a neighbor's thirty-plus live-in boyfriend to pick me up instead. When he arrived, he told me about the changes and I trusted him because our family knew him. We rode along silently for quite a while until I noticed an unfamiliar expressway name and it was not in the direction of home. Noticing the change, I asked,

"Where are we going?"

Not looking at me, he answered,

"You'll see."

Since, as children the instruction was to respect and not question adults, there were no other questions from me at this point. He drove into a wooded area and came to a stop in the clearing. It had to be about eleven at night. He seemed to be familiar with this area and parked as if there was a building or actual location. It was obviously time for another question; I asked him,

"Where are we and why are we here?"

His answer was more like a command,

"Get into the back seat."

I asked,

"Why?"

With a direct stare in my face, he repeated his instruction. Frightened and looking outside of the car I felt doomed. The moon was full and lit the area where he had parked. I knew at this point, he had taken me to a place where he knew no one would hear my cries or screams. Since I knew better than to agitate a criminal, there was no sense in being disobedient and dead, so I complied with his instruction to get into the back seat. He raped me and took me home as if it was nothing—as if he had not done anything wrong.

When we arrived, Mamma met me at the door and asked what had taken so long. Mumbling some incoherent reply, I continued up to my room remembering how little adults believed children. Experience taught me that if I told, no one would believe it. Getting into the bed, curling into the fetal position, my back facing Diana, not saying a word was my form of comfort. I had hoped that staring the blank wall, in the dark, would ease the emotional and physical pain suffered from two men trusted with my care. While my father stole my innocence, the neighbor robbed me of my virginity. A couple of day's later I finally told my brother Glenn and sister, Diana what had happened, asking them not to tell. However, time told the story—I was pregnant.

DECIDING MY LIFE AWAY

Three months went by and I began to show and told Mamma I thought I was pregnant. Mamma revealed her suspicions by saying,

"I wondered when you were going to say something,—you haven't had a menstrual cycle."

To confirm our worst fear, Mamma and I went to see a doctor. My clothes no longer fit and I did not want to go around friends or other family members—and definitely no part of this bulging stomach. Hiding my condition with a pink jacket was my solution, but probably obvious.

Around the fourth month, my stomach began to move into two different directions. I told Mamma that I thought there were two babies inside of my stomach. I even told the doctor, however, the same old thing occurred—no one believed me. In order to cause a miscarriage I attempted strenuous activities, but nothing prevailed. Then, when I arrived at the end of my solutions, God became the answer. Big Mamma Ella had taught me the Lord's Prayer and taught me to say it every night before going to bed when I was younger. I thanked God for knowing how to communicate with him through this simple prayer. The prayer began to open me up to telling God all about my troubles and everything I had been going through in my entire life.

School was no longer a place of refuge; it was a place of disgrace. My life had turned upside down and I did not know how to get out of the tailspin. Even requesting an abortion had proven to be out of the question.

One day, Mamma had run into the bathroom in a hurry. I was nearby and began talking to her through the door. I asked Mamma why she did not ask me who had fathered the baby. Mamma responded,

"It's not important—not as important as you."

I revealed the father anyway—I heard Mamma fall off the toilet. When I came into the bathroom to help her, she was holding her chest. I thought she was having a heart attack. Helping her get to her feet, she explained that it was such a shock because she had sent the rapist to me. She wanted to know why I had not told her.

"I was afraid to tell you Mamma."

She further went on to explain that she understood a lot more about why I did not reveal the crime or the predator. She attributed it to my father and his behavior toward me. She went on further to explain that it was clear I did not know how to respond to the violent act that had occurred to me.

"Denise, this rape has a lot to do with your father."

It was clear from that point on that the relationship between Mamma and my father would drastically take a turn for the worst—especially since she knew of his sick and depraved behavior.

Mamma told my father what happened and how I became pregnant. He was furious. What was even more audacious, was that he had the nerve to talk about how far under the jail the rapist should be placed. After what he had been doing to me all of my life, it was no wonder that events had happened as they did. Thinking to myself, no one is going to have me take any part of going to court and telling people what had happened to me. It would surely reveal my father, and Mamma was not going to let that happen.

The dread of Mamma telling her friend and neighbor that her boyfriend had impregnated her daughter was going to cause a big rift in their relationship. Despite the worst, Mamma told her anyway. The two women, putting their heads together, and father wanting to force him to take care of me, decided that the boyfriend and I would get married. Thinking to myself,

"Oh no—I was not about to marry a man I did not know or care about to satisfy petty gossip."

It was bad enough that this man had raped me and gotten away with the crime. However, in order to cover for him (with marriage to me) was total disregard of my feelings and extremely hurtful.

The next decision was what to do about what others thought. Here I was in a very dysfunctional state of living and yet there was concern about what others thought? The sickness of the adults in my life at this time was nearly too much to bear. Not only did I not want to live anymore, but to have the gall and nerve to want me to marry some thirty-year old something degenerate was hard to imagine. The thoughts of suicide danced in my mind regularly. Suicide had been once before the solution when I was nine. The reality of what my father was doing to me on a regular basis had finally invaded my logical mind. I felt the solution was death. It was the fall season of the year. Contemplation of suicide occurred just before my tenth birthday. The incident that drew me to this decision was an event that happened when we lived on LaSalle Boulevard. My father had called all of the children into his bedroom. He had a naked doll in his hand that belonged to Diana and me. He lifted the doll and asked who drew the artwork between the doll's legs. Naturally, all of the children denied the drawing. He instructed us all to take turns looking at the doll closely and then drawing what we saw on a piece of paper. Being naïve and thinking it was a contest where the best artist would get a prize, I became excited. I totally misunderstood his motive for the drawing. When I had finished my picture, it was nearly an exact reproduction of the vulgar artwork on the doll. Everyone else's artwork was different. Thinking I had produced the best drawing, a smile came across my face.

My father examined each of the drawings and asked Mamma which drawing matched the doll best. She replied,

"Denise."

I became so excited. There had to be a prize for doing such a good job. My father angrily looked toward me and shouted,

"Why would you do such a thing?"

I was puzzled and had no idea of what he was talking about or what he meant. Looking at both Mamma and my father totally confused, I began to speak, but was sent to my room.

"Go to your room Denise and wait for your whipping. Your Mamma will whip you good for this."

I interrupted, denying the charges.

"My picture was the best, so why am I getting a whipping?"

He responded in a nasty tone,

"The picture on the doll was wrong and it matched the drawing on the doll." Continuing to defend myself, I responded,

"You told us to draw the picture like the doll and I did what you said to do, not because I was the one who did it!"

Mamma took me to the bedroom and whipped me anyway. I remember the whipping and the pain so very well.

The next morning, the events of the former night lodged in my head as a death warrant. While walking to school my brothers, sister, and I came upon a busy intersection. My mind was set to initiate my suicide plan at this particular intersection. I was to walk out into the intersection and end my life. I waited for just the right moment. As the cars came closer I inched toward the curb, so I would go unnoticed. Finally, as a series of cars began to pass, I stepped off the curb,—Glenn's quick hand pulled me back with a hard tug as the driver screeched on his brakes. Glenn and Diana stared at me, nearly speaking in unison,

"What is the matter with you? Didn't you see that car coming?"

I just looked at them and walked across the street without looking. The driver of the car looked startled and angry at my response. At this point, I just did not care. However, now the circumstances were different and definitely more valid. Stepping off a curb would not guarantee me death. A little maturity had brought along a little knowledge. I knew the possibility of survival would still exist. Therefore, this time, it would be something more subtle. Poison would be the method of death this time. I had made the decision that if I had to go to court, my father would pursue the arrest of the rapist without me. This was the end of the line, I just could not face life anymore, and the solution of death became more appealing by the day. Death would be my escape hatch to somewhere else and I was going to enjoy the ride.

One day I shared my plans with a friend. This had to be a friend, because she told Mamma. Mamma promised me she would talk to my father about not going through with taking the incident to court or forcing marriage. Apparently, she was successful and it prevented me from fulfilling my suicide pact. However, it did not stop me from wanting to disappear or hide from society.

Mamma wanted to keep the entire story a secret to 'save face' in the neighborhood. She was so angry when she discovered that I had told someone in the neighborhood that I was pregnant. Now nearly six months pregnant with twins is something not very hard to conceal. Not only was I petite and small, my belly had grown large and obvious.

"Denise, I did not want anyone to know about this—didn't you consider that there had been plans made to handle this? You are going to the south to be with my mother until the baby come. Then you are coming back here to finish school—don't you think girl?"

I was shocked at Mamma. Not only had she yelled at me (which is something she rarely did), but she also had taken it upon herself to decide what I was going to do with these babies in my stomach. People knew I was not carrying around a tumor or a watermelon, so where was her head?

The pink jacket I had been wearing to try to conceal my condition, was getting hard to zip. I needed new clothes. In school, it was getting harder and harder to conceal the obvious. It was a fact, the hard-to-zip pink jacket and schoolbooks no longer hid my condition. One day while going up the stairs, one of my classmates noticed me and slowly said my name while gazing at my stomach. I knew she suspected my condition. I gave her the eye not to say anything aloud, and she got the message. However, the embarrassment was so great; I came home and told Mamma we had to do something. Mamma looked at me for the first time in a long time with some form of compassion. She finally spoke,

"Well Denise, you must have some thoughts, what do you want to do?" Finally, someone asked me the question I wanted to hear. I asked Mamma if I could go live with Auntie and leave school until I delivered. We talked and talked. She finally agreed that I had made a wise decision. Mamma worked out the details with Auntie and she agreed to allow me to live with her.

The excitement to live with Auntie again helped ease the series of pain that I had been experiencing. We finally got everything arranged within two weeks. I went to live with Auntie in my sixth month. I knew that Auntie would keep me encouraged and positive.

During the three months before I was due, Auntie and I became very close. Not only did I learn many things about myself, but Auntie shared her life with me as well. We spent hours talking about life and each other. It was another move and another change, but this time I felt it was the right move and the right change.

Auntie and her family lived in a three-room apartment in a second floor boarding home. Sleeping on a cot near Auntie's bed made me feel safe again. During the day, we spent time talking, knitting, playing board games, shopping, visiting, and her favorite, playing cards. Auntie taught me all types of card games. She taught me Bid Whist, Spades, Poker, Black Jack, and Go Fish. Go Fish was my favorite.

There were times when Auntie would pay me for baby-sitting, her son Eric, while she ran errands. One afternoon while we were playing cards, I became adventurous and wanted to play for money. She asked me,

"Are you sure?"

I responded,

"Yes, I'm sure, can we play for fifty cents?"

Using the baby-sitting money I earned I jumped in with both eyes opened. As Auntie pulled out her change jar, we began to play. Initially, I was winning, but then as time went on the table turned. I began losing and becoming desperate to win my baby-sitting money back. It became obvious that I would not win the money back that I had lost. Heartbroken, I asked Auntie if she would give me my money back. She explained to me that I took a risk and lost. Auntie explained that one of the consequences of gambling was the loss of the baby-sitting money. What a lesson. I did continue to play cards, but not for money.

Auntie had her own way about teaching me lifetime principles. She would allow me to participate in whatever I thought was important. She would talk to me afterwards about the outcome. Whether the outcome was victorious or not Auntie always had a favorable way of handling the situation. Her opinion of what and how I did things was very important to me. She would encourage me to do whatever I wanted to the best of my ability and always used her sayings to keep me focused. I loved her telling me 'the sky is the limit' and 'you can do it.' She told me not to let anyone stop me from achieving my dreams.

Sometimes it was Auntie's sayings that helped me make good decisions. Her words gave me hope and assurance. There was a "little" game she would play on my face. Whenever we were away from each other for a long time, Auntie would touch my forehead and say,

"*I live upstairs*",

then touching my chin she'd say,

"*and you live downstairs*",

then running her finger from my chin to my forehead, she'd continue,

"*Why don't you come up and see me sometime?*"

The little gimmick would make me laugh and giggle, and it felt good to laugh sometimes. Another one of our friendly salutations was,

"*See you later, alligator*" and I would respond to Auntie with,

"*After while crocodile.*"

When she wanted me to do something for her right away, she would promise to 'dance at my wedding with bells on.' I wasted no time in doing what she had asked. Auntie and I had so many fun times together. It seemed she had a response for every phase of our relationship. We were nearly like girlfriends. I would even comment on what she wore sometimes and she would give another one of her little adages like, "Jealousy will get you nowhere" and then laugh at me in a mocked tone.

One of the things that I thought about often when living with Auntie, was my sister Diana. I hated the idea of Diana having to face those rats alone. Diana and I maybe saw each other twice since I had left and I began to miss her. Learning what stress can do to the body was not the popular buzz like it is today. It was on December 7, the year of the pregnancy, the strangest thing happened to me. As I was sitting in the kitchen thinking about my sister Diana, my body began to shake uncontrollably. The shaking lasted in intermittent flashes for about 30 seconds. Over a few hours it continued, however, since I was alone, I stayed in one area in the house. Shortly after Auntie arrived home, blood began dripping from my mouth. Thinking I had bit my tongue, Auntie gave me a towel to wipe my face and hold up to my mouth. The blood did not stop. Checking inside of my mouth in an attempt to figure out what was causing the bleeding, she asked me whether I had hurt myself somehow. It seemed like hours trying to get my mouth to stop bleeding. Auntie telephoned her sister (who stayed a few blocks away) to inform of what was happening, asking her to come help. The shaking began again and Auntie appeared frightened. She said I was having convulsions and wanted to know whether this had ever happened to me before. I told her it began happening earlier in the day. After calling Mamma and my father, she told me we were going to the hospital. Auntie's sister Thelma arrived and went to the hospital with us. Naturally, Aunt Thelma wanted to know why I was bleeding—for the first time, I saw that Auntie did not have an answer. However, knowing Auntie the way that I did, I knew she would make the best decision for me and the babies. She told her sister she was taking no chances and going to the emergency room right away.

Since my medical complaint was obvious, immediate care was imminent. Shortly after arriving, I was "whisked" away to a bed with curtains in the emergency room. Doctors and nurses were everywhere, examining and cleaning my mouth. The doctor concluded that due to the poor condition of my teeth and the amount of cavities, the hemorrhaging was coming from tenderness in my gums. Dental care was not something we could afford apparently. After making sure I was not in any pain, the doctor had my mouth gauzed to absorb the flow of blood. It looked like the drama was over. Mamma was to call back to the hospital if I continued to have further problems. I was sent back home with Mamma and my father. The return to the house saddened me and made me wish the incident had not ever happened.

I wanted to remain with Auntie. Thinking that all the excitement was over, it was actually just beginning. After being home only a few hours, I noticed spotting when I used the toilet. Calling out to Mamma, I told her what had happened and we needed to go back to the hospital. The labor pains must have heard me, because they started en route to the hospital. The pains that I felt were unlike any other pain that I had experienced. Not knowing what to expect, I became frightened.

Arriving at the hospital a second time, the emergency team must have recognized me. They immediately took me to an examination room and asked me to lie down on the bed. Mamma stood by me with a helpless expression on her face. She could only comfort me by holding my hand. My heart beat so hard it felt as if it was coming out of my chest. I wanted everything that was happening to me to stop. When the doctor went to examine me I screamed in agony and remember squeezing Mamma's hand so tight, as if I would break her fingers. The doctor informed Mamma that I was in labor and was to be 'prepped' right away; however, Mamma could not go with me. I felt so alone and afraid. The unbearable pain overwhelmed the feelings of loneliness and fear. A nurse came in and told me that I should try to relax. She said it would not be long before I would 'deliver.' Labor lasted for seven hours. The hospital gave me a spinal tap and rolled me into the delivery room. The delivery room was cold and very unfriendly. There were several doctors and nurses surrounding me telling me to push and spread my legs at the same time. My mind raced and I comforted myself with being relieved that it was finally about to be over. I pushed and obediently did everything the medical staff instructed me to do and finally the baby came out. Then suddenly I heard a nurse shout,

"Wait, wait, there is another one."

If they had listened to me, they would not have been surprised. I told everyone that there were two babies inside of me, thus, making me right all along. I looked up to the nurse and told her,

"I told them all along that I was having two babies—no one believed me."

She brushed my hair back and patted my shoulder, as I closed my eyes with relief.

Raising my head to get a glimpse of the babies, I could see that one baby was fair-skinned and the other much darker. The nurses were washing them and cleaning their skin. I asked whether I could see them. The nurse told me that I could not see them because they needed attention right away. Both weighed under two pounds each (1 pound 11 ounces and 1 pound 9 ounces).

Within hours after the delivery, December 8, I began to hemorrhage from the mouth again and this time began vomiting blood uncontrollably. There was so much blood; even the delivery staff began to become alarmed. The last thing I remembered was finally dozing off and waking up in a private room. The nurse came in to change my bedding, making comments and asking questions while she worked.

"You are the one everyone is talking about who had the twins. What you doing having a baby? You only a baby yourself? You so tiny too—how are you going to take care of those two babies?"

While she asked all these questions in one breath, I sat there listening to her and becoming angry. She did not know my story—she does not know what has happened to me. Other nurses brought their "nose" before their brain that day. Asking silly questions and playing foolish games trying to get information from me. I wanted to go home now—get out of here and away from these people.

It was December 9, 1970, that I was informed both babies died. The feeling that came over me was indescribable. The sadness was not a normal sadness, it was strange and made me feel empty inside. I cried uncontrollably. Looking up to God, I asked Him why the babies had to die. It would not be until many years later that the answer to this question would be clear. Not having the abortion (as I begged Mamma to allow) really convinced me that the chain of events leading to the day of the babies death were all meant to be exactly as they were and that God did take the babies just as I had requested.

Innocence became a word that resided so deep in the fabric of who I was...stolen by internal and external predators.

God Was Not Finished with Me Yet

✦

Footstep Nine

Prayer after prayer did not bring those babies back. I always believed that God would take the babies in the form of a miscarriage. It was never a thought that He would allow them to get all the way here and let them die. In the end, their demise gave me a second chance, so I learned to thank God for answering prayer His way.

After a few days, it became necessary to transfer me to another area in the hospital instead of labor and delivery. Hospitalized in the new area for three weeks I continued to vomit blood. The diagnosis was that I had begun to hemorrhage after the birth and the route the blood had chosen to exit my body was through my gums. It turned out that I had hemorrhaged so heavily, that it would not be possible for the hospital to send me home in my condition. In order for my discharge, my blood count would have to improve. Mamma said that during the time I was unconscious, I nearly died.

Glancing out of the window of my hospital room, snow falling in large flakes hit the glass and vanished, as days slowly passed. My 16th birthday was approaching and I wanted to go home. Mamma told me the doctor was not sure if I would be able to go home before Christmas. The hospital had become tiring and boring. Mamma explained to me that I was still in a weakened condition. She visited, smiling every day. Auntie would come every few days to see about me and paid for a television in my room. I missed my brothers and sister. It was lonely and barren in the hospital. I would look out the window at night and watch the lights for entertainment. Mamma would always leave just before nightfall. About the second week of my stay in the hospital, I met another long-term patient. We began visiting each other's room for company. At night, the nurse would give us medication that would make us giggle and laugh, but very sleepy. We would fight the sleep to enjoy the sensation of the laughter. We would walk down the hallways giggling and staggering. The nurses would get after us night after night about making noise. We enjoyed smiling and being happy so we tried to refrain from causing any trouble. The sensation gave us both the feeling of being far away and having nothing to worry about, so we took advantage of having a happy moment taking the pills. Even though I wanted to go home, I did not want to go to my home with Mamma and my father, I wanted to go back and live with Auntie.

HOME AT LAST

Despite my desires, it was home release to Mamma and my father, which occurred. Arriving at home, all I could think about was seeing Diana. It was a relief to see her after my long absence. The first thing we talked about was the girl I met in the hospital. The babies had not entered into the conversation. I did not want to contaminate our reunion with the sad part of life I experienced with the childbirth and then death of the twins. Diana and I cuddled up that night to thank the Lord for being together again. We cuddled so many times as sisters other nights to protect each other.

The next day I spent a lot of time with my brothers. We caught up on all that I had missed. School was out and the festive holiday season allowed reunion and recuperation for me. It had been nearly two months that I had been away from home. We did not get much for Christmas that year. However, it was strange that our father received quite a few presents. He had wanted a trench coat this Christmas. With all the financial problems it seemed the family had been going through, it was quite odd that he had one under the tree. Mamma suspected that one of his many girlfriends had given him the coat as a gift. We learned that from the argument that ensued in the bedroom and volume of the conversation. Our father had more gifts than we did at Christmas. He had bought us all one outfit each. We were disappointed that year that he had so much and we had so little. He actually seemed to gloat that he had the most presents. It was clear that his life outside of home had become more important in his life than our family.

BACK-TO-SCHOOL

Christmas break was over and according to the doctor; it was still too early in my weakened state to return with the other children in the house. However, during the second week of school after the first of the New Year, I returned anyway. Missing nearly two months of school meant a lot of make-up assignments and patience from the instructors. The ninth grade math teacher was not empathetic at all about helping me to catch-up. He even made a comment telling me that it was my fault for what had happened to me. His comment made me feel ashamed. I did not realize that anyone at school knew about my giving birth. I guess Mamma had to tell what happened in order to get me back into school.

Despite the obstacles, the contribution of other teachers and students who cared about me made the difference. The time went by quickly and I successfully caught up with the work missed. The adjustment was so fast, before I knew it I was in the tenth grade. By the time I reached the eleventh grade, we were on the move again. This time we moved to a home on Burchill Court in Detroit. Fortunately, we did not have to change schools and were still able to see Auntie regularly. Life seemed to be normal for a while; yet, this is how I learned that God was not finished with me yet.

"Kicking, scratching, and screaming took me into another world—the world of protecting myself from my internal predator."

Internal Predator

✦

Footstep Ten

In my short life, I had learned to live with external as well as internal predators. The internal predators could not be ran away from or avoided. There was a day Mamma went out to run errands in which my father, Edward came home again, drunk. Diana and I were the only two home and we looked at each other when he arrived knowing the worst of this 'not-so-ideal' situation. We were upstairs in the bedroom. Father called out to me,

"Denise, Denise."

Diana and I looked at each other in fear and disgust. It was the fall season before my eighteenth birthday. Answering,

"Yes", he instructed me to come see what he wanted.

We knew all too well why he had called me and what he wanted. When he saw both of us there, he made it clear that he did not want both of us to come, just me.

"Daddy, what do you want?" I blurted out to disturb the tension.

His response was to tell Diana to go upstairs and return to our bedroom. There was so much intensity in the room the air felt tight and choking. Courage left my throat again,

"Diana, don't go", and then, Diana turning to my father in a stern and firm voice, asked,

"What do you want with Denise?"

It was clear that he was surprised, even in his drunken stupor, at the boldness of the question. He responded,

"None of your business—just get upstairs like I told you!"

I did not want to get Diana into any trouble, so I motioned to her to stand by the stairs out of sight with a hand signal. I slowly walked into his bedroom to see what he wanted. Having a good idea of what he wanted...I cautiously made the last step toward the middle of the room that would clear the door. He immediately shut the door with instructions for me to lie down on the bed. I refused. Facing him, I said,

"You will never touch me again."

Ignoring my stance, he snatched me and threw me down onto the bed. Screaming as loud as I could to get Diana's attention (while fighting him off) the fight for my dignity began. Diana ran into the room and started pulling our father away from me while telling him to leave me alone. Father grabbed Diana and attempted to push her out of the room. For the first time, he had a battle on his hands. He began tussling and fighting with us. He would push down one of us, and the other would get up, pushing, and shoving until released. Pleas and cries while we were fighting him were totally ignored. The distance between the door and the bed was very short; therefore, he could hold one of us with one hand, while pushing on the other.

Nevertheless, we fought despite the insurmountable strength he had on both of us. Eventually, our father won the tug-of-war and pushed Diana out of the room. After physically locking Diana out, he commenced to do his "dirty" deed. He began pulling my clothes off while spitting out justification for his actions.

"You got pregnant with a baby—now you are a woman and having sex with you should be no problem. I can do what I want with you now."

It was so unconceivable that my own father was saying these words to me. His words made me even angrier and more determined for him to 'not have his way' with me. The fight to thwart his rape efforts intensified. I fought like never before. Kicking, scratching, and screaming took me into another world—the world of protecting myself from my internal predator. Despite his strength, I kept fighting. He grabbed both of my wrists and pinned me down. I began to use my legs and kick him wherever and however I could. He slapped me across my face so hard while telling me to be quiet; he only heightened my determination. He pushed his weight down between my legs. Each time he would try to prepare himself for penetration, I would twist my body from beneath him, forcing him to release one of my wrists. I would hit him and he would slap me again. He could not stop his sick and perverse body from getting excited from the struggle. I tired him out so from fighting that he became weak by his own lust. With one good push, I was able to kick my father from atop of me. He fell back onto the bed. Lying there exhausted and breathing heavily, he ejaculated. The sight of the act was disgusting and nauseous. There were so many feelings of disgust and realization happening at the same time, the only thing I could think of was to get my sister who had been banging on the door the whole while. When I opened the door, Diana quickly grabbed me and we ran upstairs to our bedroom crying and holding each other. Diana wanted to go back downstairs and kill him. Holding her tight and through my sobbing, told her he was not worth it. Cleaning myself up, changing clothes and combing my hair brought me back into a state of action versus hostility. Diana and I promised we would not tell Mamma when she got home. If we had, our father may very well have been dead that day. We did not tell anyone. We did not seek help. We were so use to no one believing us, keeping silent became normal. Besides, when things like this happened in your home, you were not supposed to tell anyone.

Diana and I did make a promise to each other that dreadful day. We promised that every time our father would make such an attempt, we would fight harder and use greater force to protect ourselves. Now that we were no longer helpless little girls, he was not going to do what he wanted with our bodies. We did not know where Mamma was that day, but our plans were set and minds made up to do whatever it took to fight our father and his demented plans. It was frightening not knowing what to expect from father each day—he seemed to have many faces.

WHO IS TO BLAME?

Mamma was beginning to change. It seemed as if the rape by the neighbor had made her feel as if someone had to take the blame. Resuming my life as if nothing happened bothered her. Part of starting over meant learning to become independent. One of the local high schools offered driver's training, and I had signed up for the course. In order to get to the school, it would mean traveling by bus to the other side of town. We would let Mamma know where we were at all times. This particular day I called Mamma and told her I had just arrived for driver's training. When she answered the phone, I could tell she had been drinking. We engaged in a discussion about me having permission to attend the class this particular day. Despite being disappointed and angry, I agreed to come home. Once home, Mamma was sitting in the dining room. Sitting down near her, I asked her,

"Why did you have me come home and you knew it was my drivers training day?"

We began to argue. Words and comments began to flare. Mamma began saying cruel and vicious things to me she had never said before. She even made a remark about the rape. I responded by questioning,

"What does the rape have to do with driver's training?"

She came back with some half-baked reason related to what others would think about me. Her suggestion was that I should be ashamed of being active. Responding to her strongly, I commented,

"I am going to live my life and nothing is going to stop me."

By this time, Diana had come down the stairs. She stopped by the bottom of the staircase, which leads directly into the dining room. I guess Mamma felt that Diana was going to jump in and defend me. Mamma grabbed my jacket collar and began to hit me. Eventually, Diana did exactly what Mamma thought she would do. I spoke up and told Mamma to leave us both alone. She slurred out that I could leave and take Diana with me. We practically ran out of the door. My brothers were in the house. Diana and I did not want the incident to go any further, so we ran to avoid more trouble.

REALIZATIONS

The night was cold and very dark. It was about eight o'clock that night with seventy-five cents between the two of us, and we had eaten no dinner.

We walked the neighborhood going from one schoolmate to another asking someone to let us spend the night. No one was able to accommodate us, but one family did give us a dollar so we could travel to the west side of Detroit. Diana was very cold. She had left the house without a coat. We were sharing my coat. We finally caught the bus to the west side of town. We went to a friend's house to see whether we could stay the night. She told us we should leave. Diana and I continued our search. Visiting another friend brought about the same answer, however, we did gain a coat for Diana. Finally, we found a friend that would take us in for the night a few blocks from where Auntie lived. About twenty minutes went by and we heard a knock. I told our host that if it was somebody looking for us, we were not there. As sure as if, I seen through the door, it was a cousin. We stayed until about two o'clock in the morning but could stay no longer—we had to leave. After leaving, we walked a few blocks to where Auntie lived. Naturally, she was glad to see us and shared with us that everyone was worried. She immediately called our father and told him where we were. She asked him to let us stay until the next day. Our father said,

"No—I will be there to get them right away."

Shortly, Mamma and our father arrived to get us. Mamma, still very much intoxicated began to rant and rave about how if we did not like what she said or did, that it was too bad, and we still had the option to leave home. Our father looked at her and told her to be quiet. He pointed toward the door and told us to get into the car. We rode home in silence. Once arriving home, the only good thing about it was we were out of the cold. Running away from home and not having shelter was not a choice we made anymore. Even though Mamma and father had drinking and fighting issues, they also had heat.

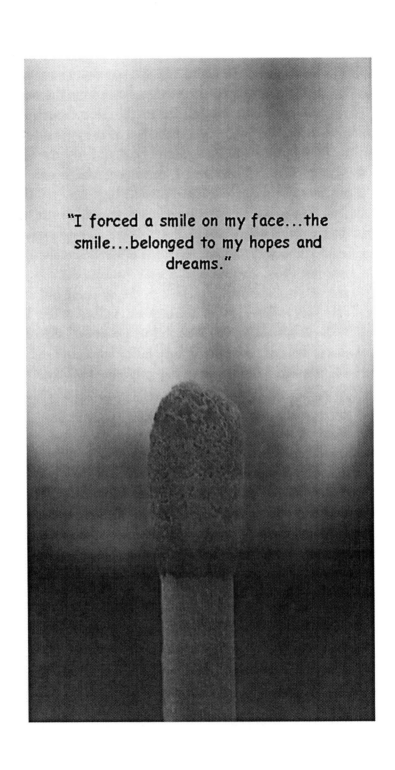

"I forced a smile on my face...the smile...belonged to my hopes and dreams."

Dickerson Street

✦

Footstep Eleven

We were on the move again. This time we moved from Burchill Court to Dickerson Street. Our father was rarely around these days. Since the incident where Diana and I stood up to him, he found home as a place only to lay his head. There were occasional times he would entertain friends, but that was it. The pivotal days as a senior in high school, designed for excitement and high anticipation, were not. Money was scarce, alcoholism high, and graduation gifts few. I did not get to attend senior activities and program events. Mamma wanted to help, but could not, due to the lack of funds. Our father had stopped helping us out financially a long time before my senior year. However, it was during this very important time in my life, my father's changes reared its ugly head. Pleading with my father for five dollars to have my senior picture taken, only to have the check "bounce" was like adding salt to a wound. It hurt not having my picture in the yearbook. Disappointment followed my senior year like a plague. Not only had I been left out of major events, the graduation event was even worst. My father did not attend. I had no money or new outfit like the other graduating students.

After commencement, friends were going out shopping and eating to celebrate. Tagging along, I forced a smile on my face that I had worn most of my high school years. The smile did not actually belong to me; the smile belonged to my hopes and dreams. Keeping an upbeat attitude kept ambition and goals high in a very unhappy childhood. The major goal in my life was to attend college, secure a doctorate degree, and retire financially at age 45. In order to meet those goals college had to be on the agenda.

Michigan State University was my college of choice. In 1973, having my orientation invitation in hand, and again, another dream squashed by my father. He would not complete the financial aid papers. In order to file paperwork for financing, income tax information was required. Because my father had not filed for previous tax years, he was afraid of penalties and repercussions of his neglect, he was not filling out the paperwork. When questioned about whether my education was more important than his tax penalty payments, he clearly stated—the penalties! His reaction threw me into a "fit" of anger. Expressing my dissatisfaction to his reply led me to standing on my "soap box" and letting him know that I was going to make it and his lack of cooperation was not going to stop me.

Mamma stood close by listening to the conversation. There was a sad and pitiful look on her face. My father stormed out the door as I flung myself into a kitchen chair and began to sob. Placing my head into my hands and crying seemed to be the only comfort at the time. Thinking as I cried, it was clear that something had to change. Yes indeed, something positive in my life was far overdue.

OPPORTUNITY RANG A BELL

The summer days in Detroit could get very hot and the sun would shine very bright. A few weeks had passed since the time my father had affirmed his lack of support in my interest towards college. The clang of a local ice cream vendor alerted me to another direction. This particular day it was very hot. Not only was the vendor selling soft-swirled ice cream, but he was also offering an opportunity. He was asking the young children coming for ice cream whether or not they knew anyone 18 years of age that was looking for a job. He needed some assistance and they would be riding with him on the ice cream truck. His only preference was that it would need to be a male.

I was hanging clothes in the backyard with Mamma when I first heard about the job offer. One of the neighbor girls ran into the backyard excited and nearly exhausted asking me whether I wanted to work on an ice cream truck. Between huffs and puffs, she rattled out the details. I was able to determine that "18 years old" was the critical element to determine employment. Not only had this young girl brought the information, she had also asked him to wait. Gasping and pulling me at the same time, she hurried me toward the truck. She was so excited, as if she knew it was my job.

After speaking with the vendor, he wanted me to start immediately. He was so impressed with my enthusiasm and quick understanding of what was required, it did not matter that I was female. A job rolled through my neighborhood and I was available to make the move. Running back to the house, I explained everything to Mamma as calmly as I could. Everything happened so fast, the hours, the pay, and what I would be doing tumbled from my lips. He wanted me to start immediately. Mamma agreed to let me work.

It took me about three weeks to learn the operation as a vendor assistant. The hours were from 9:00am until 9:00pm, Monday through Saturday. Sundays, the shift was from 1:00pm to 9:00pm. Soon, I became the first female employee with a truck to operate and manage. Earnings from the truck helped Mamma run the household. Edward, our father, had abandoned his family. Mamma was doing all she could to care for us and keep the household together. She had a part-time job at a nearby school as an assistant working with mentally and physically challenged children. Mamma enjoyed helping the children and would sometimes take care of them in our home. During my elementary and middle school years, Mamma would do this type of work and had experience to move into the part-time job easily.

Driving the ice cream truck and having money to contribute to the household gave me a sense of independence. The owner of the five-truck operation was pleased that I had become the largest moneymaking driver. The entire operation grossed anywhere from $700.00 (considered a bad week) to $1500 (considered a good week) per week. Our prime clientele were the children purchasing ice cream cones that cost fifteen to twenty cents. The younger children were the primary consumers. Nearly doubling and sometimes tripling what other drivers were grossing enabled me to recruit my two younger brothers and a male neighbor. Before turning in the truck for the day, I would stop by the house and give Mamma and Auntie a treat of ice cream on me.

Now that our household had seemed to regulate, Auntie had started coming back over more regularly. It was always clear that Auntie and Mamma were very close. Auntie had birthed her second child, who turned out to be a girl born on August 4, 1972. She would come over often with her children. Now that our life seemed to be coming together, we laughed more and enjoyed each other's company in our home. Harmony and happiness dominated during this hot summer in July. I stopped selling ice cream mid September of 1973. It was time for life to make another turn.

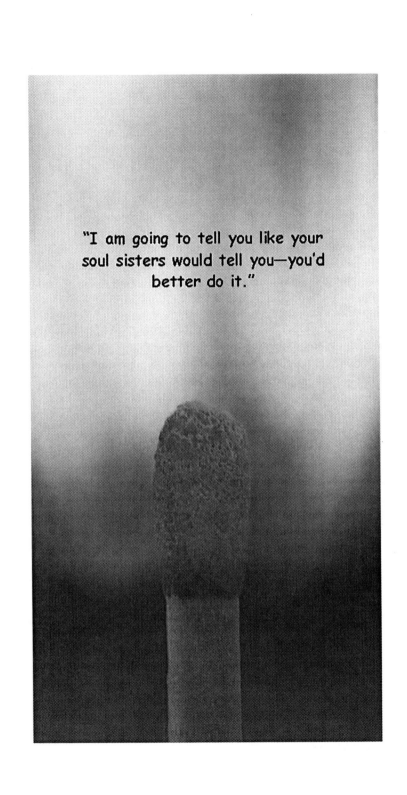
"I am going to tell you like your soul sisters would tell you—you'd better do it."

Fire Works!

✦

Footstep Twelve

The fall of 1973 brought about many new changes in my life. Now that my successful stint with ice cream vending was over, it was now time to get back to original lifetime goals. I enrolled in a private downtown Detroit business college and began to look for long-term employment. Mamma would still need help with the household budget, and I wanted to continue to help her. The relationship with Auntie had begun to become more consistent as I visited her, (using public transportation) and would sometimes bring her children to my house.

Late spring of 1974 brought about yet more changes. I had to curtail attending business college due to misleading information related to registration. Since I needed employment to help the family survive, it seemed only logical to put off school one more time. Employment came through working the afternoon shift at a small automotive parts supplier plant in Fraser, Michigan. The job entailed racking parts for Chrysler vehicles, mainly door handles. As time went by, my leadership skills rose to the top once more. The supervisor offered me piece bonus work. Having become the fastest parts 'racker' and leader for the afternoon shift, I took the offer gladly. Not only did I need the money, but also because of the high turnover rate, I was able to recruit members of my family. The recruitment did not stop with my family. I also recruited several neighbors including Mamma's best friend. All of us worked together on the afternoon shift, and all of us were women. The work was strenuous and hard on our backs. Each worker had to get parts from a large bin and place them in to a small crate. Then we would lift the crate and carry it back to the work area. Each rack held about 50 door handles. Next, the filled racks' next stage was to be rolled into a waiting area for the male employees to steel plate the handles. The racks would then be lifted, by a hanger, and immersed into a plating boiler. The working conditions in the plant were undesirable, to say the least. The plant was extremely hot, dusty, not well ventilated, and we ate lunch in the 'ladies room'. There was nowhere else to eat. The plant was a very dangerous place to work. It was so dangerous that a worker on the day shift fell into the boiler one day and met his death. Employment at this job would be short-lived, to say the least.

In addition to the danger of the job, the shift supervisor had very little people skills. He was especially non-tactful toward black employees. On the afternoon shift, it was clear that the supervisor had definite lines of distributed work duties. It seemed that the black women would perform all of the labor-intensive duties, while white female counterparts would inspect. The males, all-white, would perform the semi-skilled plating functions. There were no black male employees on the afternoon shift. At the end of the shift, the black women were to clean and sweep the plant before going home, while our white counterparts only packed up their things and left for the day. The cleaning duties rotated only among the black employees.

TIME TO SPEAK UP

When the time came for me to do the sweeping, I informed the supervisor that due to allergies, the dust would make breathing difficult for me if I were to sweep. The supervisor offered no dust mask but instead placed his finger in my face and yelled,

"I am going to tell you like your soul sisters would tell you—you'd better do it."

Mamma heard him and immediately came toward the sound of the threat and my defense. A couple of other women came with Mamma over to where I was, they knew something I did not know—Mamma was intoxicated. Mamma got into the supervisor's face and the yelling match began. Workers began pulling Mamma away from the supervisor. They attempted to defend the inability for me to sweep the floor. Finally, the supervisor threw his last threat at them saying,

"You are all going to be fired if the floor is not swept—so make your decision and get out of my face."

Two workers took my place and quickly swept the plant floor. Since there was no union, we just took things in stride until we could do better.

Early summer it became evident that we could no longer take the abusive tone and manner in which we (female black laborers) were treated. There was obvious discrimination and preferential job treatment. Soon the Fourth of July holiday came—discrimination became the issue once more. The black employees maintained a work schedule while white female employees had the day off. Despite being paid double time, we viewed the action as unfair, because we too wanted to be home with our families for the holiday.

Since I was the leader on the afternoon shift, I shared with the supervisor how the employees felt about having to work the holiday. He scoffed and flung out a remark that if anyone were absent, would mean immediate release. Taking back to the employees the comment, (which included the supervisor being unwilling to change his mind), and the immediate dismissal threat, brought about comments and anger. It seemed that the only way to make a stand was to leave willingly. After questioning the employees on whether they had enough money to survive and look for other employment, a hand vote determined our fate. I instructed everyone to get their belongings and punch out. The supervisor approached me angrily asking me,

"What's going on?"

I responded,

"Well, since you are not a soul sister, I really don't think you would understand."

Punching out my time card, I laughed and walked out. None of us ever went back.

With $100.00 and no job, I decided to catch the bus and visit my grandparents in Georgia. Needing to clear my mind and get ready for the next move in my life, required peace and quiet. The silence and peace lasted for only a few days. Big Mamma informed me that Mamma was very ill with food poisoning and taken to the hospital. Catching the next Greyhound bus to Detroit, I found myself connecting on a city bus to the house. Approaching the house, seven houses from the corner, I saw Mamma sitting in her upstairs bedroom staring out of the window. We looked at each other. With relief that she was home, I quickly ran into the house to her. As she turned away from the window to meet my greeting, we looked at each other again with endearing eyes. After a moment of silence, I finally allowed the words to leave my mouth,

"Mamma, are you all right?"

There was something more than food poisoning going on in her mind. I went on to ask her why was she so sad and what had caused her to just look out of the window as she was doing…she looked very depressed. Slowly lifting her eyes away from me toward the window, she spoke the words that must have broken her heart.

"Your father has divorced me."

She said she had not told anyone except me. Reaching under her mattress to show me the divorce decree, her hands shook and then steadied as she placed the document into my hands. Despite me taking her into my arms and holding her, whispering promises of taking care of her, an immediate display of concern was not enough. The penetration of the pain she was feeling had entered into a deep portal of her mind. Mamma was thankful for my comfort, but it was clear, my reaction did not ease her pain.

As Mamma went on into discussion about the divorce, she uncovered the deeper part of her pain. Leaving her and the children was a clear indicator that the divorce would follow; however, she was dismayed because the divorce decree allowed her no alimony or custody of the minor children. She invested nearly 17 years of her life to raising us and left with nothing and no one except her memories. All she had to show for the marriage was an unfaithful man who had left her for another woman.

Mamma said she knew about other women in my father's life for years, but he could have at least left her with custody of the youngest boys. She thought he would be fair. She continued to tell me that we were all she had in life. Since she was not our biological mother, the court told her that she had no custodial rights. Mamma explained that our father probably did it on purpose, so that he would not have to give any money for them. The whole nightmare of what our father did to Mamma, made me angry. Encouraging Mamma to fight him brought an unexpected response.

"I am too tired to fight, it's too late, and I should have begun this fight a long time ago."

It was clear from the look on Mamma's face that she meant every word of what she spoke.

"I could have left your father many years ago with nothing personal to lose, but I stayed because of you children. All of you needed a mother."

Mamma had tears in her eyes all the time she spoke. The whole situation became worse. Despite the language of the divorce decree, our father had laid another burden upon Mamma.

"Edward has refused to take the two younger boys to live with him and his new woman."

Mamma spoke with apparent remorse. The boys remained with Mamma and she accepted the result as a means to remain with us. This new information really made me furious. Mamma was weak and tired, but I was young and willing to take on the fight. Pleading with Mamma, I asked her to take us all to court and fight. Mamma softly said,

"The only thing that matters to me now is that I have all of you with me. The Lord will provide a way for us."

"I hate him, I hate him," I screamed.

Mamma told me not to say things like that and no matter what my father did, it was nothing in hate that would make it change.

"Yeah, some father", I said.

Mamma said that before our father leaves this world that he was going to suffer and call on me for help. She told me I should go and see about him and the Lord would bless me for my actions. My heart ached for Mamma.

Just as we finished our conversation, Grandmother Ella telephoned that my best friend, Ida, who I had just visited in Georgia, had been murdered by her boyfriend hours before I got on the bus. I was told that he had been physically abusing her and thought she was out with another man, so he stripped her naked and beat her to death in the middle of the road. I felt as if someone had reached into my chest and taken my heart out. Listening to Mamma and now Ida, it was almost too much for me to bear at the same time. Ida and I had been friends since the age of five. We would have so much fun together each time I visited Georgia. She lived next door to my grandmother Ella. Ida and a couple of her girlfriends had taken me to the drive-in for the late night showing since I had just arrived in Georgia. After the show, they dropped me at my grandmother's house at approximately 1:15 a.m. Ida's murder took place at approximately 3:00 a.m.

When I went to bed that night, I shared the conversation I had with Mamma and about Ida with my sister Diana. My pillow full of tears became my best friend that night. I waited until morning before telling my brothers. We were all bitter and angry at what our father had done to Mamma. We begin, one-by-one to express our anger toward our father.

Unfortunately, Mamma thought she could drown the pain in alcohol and had begun to drink more regularly. She began to argue more and show her bitterness. Her actions did not discourage me from wanting to help her with taking care of the household needs.

Somewhere along the way, Mamma met a man who enjoyed drinking as she did. He was not someone we particularly liked having around, but he was Mamma's friend. One night he visited, and was upstairs in the bedroom talking with Mamma. Making a comment to Diana about him being there (and in Mamma's bedroom), apparently was overheard by Mamma. She approached the doorway of my room and asked me to come out into the hallway. It was clear that she had been drinking. She and I began to get into a heated discussion about the man being there. She became even more upset and began to lash out at me. Mamma had not ever made an attempt like this to hit me before. When I tried to pull away, she grabbed my arm and bit me as hard as she could. It was obvious that her anger was not towards me but towards father. I endured the pain, without a whimper, as I looked into her hurting eyes. Everyone, even her male friend forced her to stop biting me. When they were finally able to detach my arm from her, there was a large bite mark left on my forearm, which had begun to swell. Refusing to cry, I pretended as if it did not hurt. Running into the bathroom, I ran cold water on the area. The love for

Mamma took over my good senses, since I did not go for medical treatment, my forearm stayed swollen for many days. The bite mark looked awful and it took 3-4 weeks for it to disappear.

It was not long after the incident with Mamma, that I took a part-time job at a men's clothing store with my brother Glenn. I still wanted to help Mamma with the bills. Around the second week in August 1974, after arriving home from work, my youngest brother was sitting on the porch with a sad and confused look on his face. I asked him what was wrong. He told me something that completely caught me by surprise...he told me Mamma was gone.

"What do you mean gone?" "Gone, where?" I said.

She was indeed gone. Rushing into the house, I noticed that furniture was missing as well as the refrigerator. Panicking I began going through the entire house to see what other things were missing. Returning to Lonny, I asked him how long had he been home. He explained that she was gone when he arrived home. I began to canvass the neighbors asking whether they knew anything. Surely, one of them would tell me what had happened. No one was talking.

After everyone came home for the day, I questioned all of my brothers and sister to ask whether they knew anything and they too knew nothing about Mamma leaving or planning to leave. There was not a note or anything for us to know where she had gone. I even called our father, who made the remark, "She had better get back there and take care of you kids." Talking to him was like talking to a brainless idiot. When I explained that it was obvious that she had left, he still did not comprehend what had occurred. When I explained that, we did not have food or a refrigerator, he responded that we were old enough to take care of ourselves. It left me feeling as our family was 'thrown' away. Glenn and I began adding up the money we had on hand so that we could buy some food. Our sister Diana was pregnant and close to delivery, Lonnie and Michael were still attending school. Ernest came and went and we could not contact him. We knew we had to take the reins of our family and stay together. It was a trying time that we had to face—once more.

"Living in a lie for over 17 years had convinced Mamma that her love for our father would stand the test of time, yet it did not survive his lack of love."

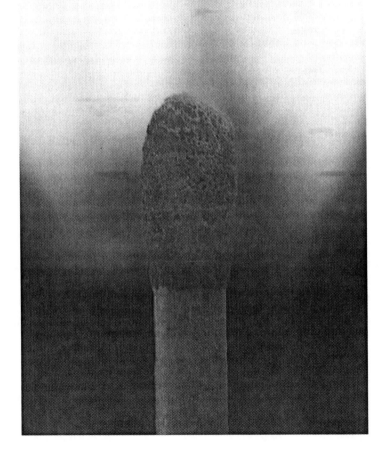

Living a Lie

◆

Footstep Thirteen

A week had passed since Mamma had left. We lived seven days without knowing what had happened to cause her to leave. Finally, one of the neighbors across the street informed us that Mamma had moved to Alabama with her male friend. She told the neighbor that she did not want anyone to let us know until she had arrived safely and settled down. The neighbor told us that Mamma would call us sometime the following week.

It was about 7:00pm the following week, just as was told to us, when Mamma called wanting to speak with me. Lonny answered the phone and handed it to me. As I placed the phone to my ear, my sister and brothers looked at me as I began. I slowly spoke as calmly as I could,

"Hello, Mamma, where are you?"
Before she could answer, I started telling her all that had happened since she left.

"We don't have any food and daddy is not helping us with anything. Why did you leave us?"
The barrage of questions started pouring out of my mouth like a broken cistern. The conversation began to sound like a parent scolding their child. Mamma responded calmly,

"Denise, I had to get away. I had done all I could and your father left me no other choice but to find my way in life."
She continued,

"It's time for me to have a little happiness now. All of you are strong children, and you have gone through a lot, so I know how strong you

all are. I could not legally adopt you and there was no other way but for
me to leave for all of our good."

It was clear in Mamma's voice that she was heart-broken and sad about
what had occurred; however, it was something that she had to do for herself. It was not just enough to be a good mother physically. There were no
legal ties between Mamma and us. Living in a lie for over 17 years had
convinced Mamma that her love for our father would stand the test of
time, yet, it did not survive his lack of love. Despite the love lost between
Mamma and our father, the love for us remained. The unconditional love
she showed us is what kept her holding on to a hopeless marriage. In her
conversation, she revealed to me that she had met someone that we could
not accept. We had told Mamma that he was not "good enough" for her.
Mamma decided that she could not allow us to interfere with the little
happiness she had found in this man. With a confident and clear voice, she
paused and spoke directly to her faith in me as the caretaker of my family.

"Denise, she said, "I know I can depend on you to take care of your
brothers and sister. You are strong. Of all of my children, you are the
least that I worry about as far as being 'all right'. You are a fighter Denise, and I know you will see to everything."

She paused again. Returning to speaking about all of us, Mamma went on
to say,

"I love all of you very much. No matter what happens to me, please
promise me that you will see to the needs of your Aunt Catherine.
Without her help, I could not have taken care of you all as I did all of
those years. You know what she has done for you. Promise me that if
Aunt Catherine needs anything, that you will take care of it."

With my head tilted down and then quickly up to the phone in an upbeat
tone, I assured her,

"I promise Mamma. We love you", and hung up the phone.

In those last moments on the phone, it was as if Mamma and I could
see each other's eyes. It was as if our hearts felt each other's beat and the
rhythm of the suffering echoed in the words that she could not speak. My
heart was hurting, but not for me. My heart was in pain for all of the suffering that Mamma suffered with my father, just to love us.

Each child stood eagerly waiting for our conversation to end, wanting to know what Mamma had said and why she had left. Innocence and love kept the question on their lips,

"When is Mamma coming back?"

Taking the reins of the family, I arched my back and looked at each one of them, scanning from each tender face and said,

"Mamma loves us very much, but now it is time for us to take care of ourselves."

Further instruction came into my tone,

"Don't hold anything against Mamma; she had to do what she did for herself. She owed this time to herself."

A mild wave of silence entered the room, as if everyone mourned the loss of a death, but picked up their heads and began to ask planning questions. It was as if they were content with my response and had been convinced to get to the task of survival. That is exactly what we did.

NEW HEADS OF THE HOUSEHOLD

Approximately three weeks after Mamma left, Glenn, and I continued working and providing for the family. Lonny and Mike were continuing their schooling and not missing a day. Diana, in her final stages of pregnancy, stayed home took care of herself and the house. We had a plan. The plan worked until Diana had the baby August 28, 1974. Money and food became scarce. The winter was approaching early and we had received a copy of a 90-day eviction notice, previously mailed to Mamma. The house was in foreclosure. An eviction date of November 23, 1974 had been set. We were living in a house that was in foreclosure. We had no money and nowhere to go. We had become the new heads of the household. With the new baby to feed and clothe, things really became tough. During the evenings and weekends, Glenn and I would look for a new place to live. Glenn and I would catch the bus on a daily basis hoping to find another place to live further away and in a nicer neighborhood. Fortunately, Glenn and I were paid weekly.

Glenn and I met denial after denial. We became weary of hearing the same response—

"You're just children; we are not renting to kids. Kids party and make trouble; we don't want trouble, besides they don't pay their rent either."
Landowners would deny us; no matter what Glenn and I would say to try to convince them of our maturity. However, Glenn and I would faithfully go out one more day.

Auntie would visit when she could, considering she had two small children, she continued to watch over us. Time was running out and winter made the early entry we had anticipated. It became harder to pay the heating bills, buy food, formula, and keep the baby in diapers with the income we had between Glenn and me. Lonny and Mike needed coats, boots, and gloves. We even became desperate enough to ask our father for help. To no great surprise, he said,

"No."
We continued to wonder why this man showed no compassion for his own blood. One day I became angry about his constant refusal to help us. Remembering what Mamma had told me about our father having legal custody" of Lonny and Mike. I told the younger boys to pack their bags because they were going to their father. Since he had "legal custody", he should take "legal responsibility" for his minor children. Lonny and Mike did not understand and did not want to go. I assured them that I loved them and this was the only way I could provide food and a roof over their heads.

After getting a ride to our father's house, Glenn and I reached our destination about nine in the evening on a cold and brisk Michigan night. There was snow on the ground and our breath was visible in the cold night air. Our father must have been at work, and his new wife was not answering the door. Determined not to leave without accomplishing our goal, I knocked on the lower flat door to get the attention of our father's stepdaughter who lived in the flat beneath my father and his new wife. When she opened the door I did not wait for her to invite me in, I just stepped into the doorway with my brothers in tow. Quickly asking her whether her mother was home, she guided me through her flat and up the back stairs to where the couple lived.

When father's wife opened the door, I walked right in with an attitude saying, "Here are daddy's two sons. It is his right and responsibility to take care of them—not mine. Their clothes are in the paper bags." My poor brothers looked scared clinging tightly to the brown paper bags, which held their few belongings. Looking lost for words, father's wife ran hastily to the telephone. Knowing that she was calling my father, and caring less, I walked pass her, out of the front door and down the stairs. Glenn was waiting in the car. We sped off into the darkness.

After catching my breath, my heart began to ache at the thought of Lonny and Mike not being somewhere that would be a true home. I just did not know what else to do. Returning home, I called Auntie and told her what I had done. She bluntly told me,

"Your father is not going to keep them there."

I responded loudly,

"He better keep them there. He better not send them back."

Auntie comforted me that everything was going to be all right. I eventually went to bed, but did not sleep well. Just thinking about whether Lonny and Mike were angry with me for leaving them with our father was like torture.

The next morning I went to work feeling uneasy. Calling home to check on the baby and Diana to make sure they were alright, Diana told me that Lonny and Mike were back home. Our father had brought them home earlier and was very angry when he walked in the house. He wanted to know where I was and left a threatening message with Diana.

"If Denise brings Lonny and Mike back over to my house, I will put my foot so up her a—, that it will come out of her mouth."

Shocked and angry that he would leave such a vile message with my sister, I came home from work. The message was clearly upsetting to Diana, so I knew I had to do some damage control at home to keep everyone together. Once I reached home, I immediately apologized to Lonny and Mike. I explained to them that I thought the act would prompt our father into taking care of them. After soothing them and giving them huge hugs, I asked them to leave the room. I did not want them to hear what I was about to say to our father.

Dialing the telephone, a dialog of a lifetime went like this—

"Hello, Daddy, this is Denise. I got your message."

Our father responding,

"I'm glad you did. I meant every bit of what I said."

We went on in a heated conversation and then in a calmer and civiler tone, I continued,

"Since you won't take care of us and not even provide us with a morsel of bread, until we are evicted, the house is mine, and I am the head of the household. Should you ever step foot in my house or anywhere on my property I would find you and "blow your head off "—we don't need you—God will take care of us."

He laughed and hung up the phone. When the conversation was over, I instructed everyone on not letting our father anywhere near the house and if he came anyway to call me. I immediately telephoned Auntie after talking with the other children. As always, Auntie gave me words of encouragement. She told me that God was really going to bless me one day for the responsibility I had taken on in caring for my sister and brothers. Her words echoed not only in my mind, but also in my spirit, when she told me,

"What you are doing is a big thing in the eyes of God. Don't let your father get the best of you."

Michigan winter was showing its strength. The days and nights were bitter cold. I had become concerned about Michael and Lonny's trek to school. The bus ride was long and they did not have proper clothing. Once again, I telephoned daddy for help and met with the same response as before. My knowing that they needed proper clothing, I went to Social Services for help but denied because I was not their legal guardian. One day upon discovering Lonny's hands nearly frost bitten after returning home from school and Michael complaining of cold feet, I knew something had to be done. Glenn and I discussed the matter but we did not have enough money to buy them the coat, gloves, and boots they needed so badly. Faced with the dreadful situation of seeing our brothers suffer, Glenn and

I looked at each other as if we were reading each other's mind. We held our heads knowing we had come to the same conclusion. Through our despair, both of us entertained thoughts that were totally against our 'home training' and beliefs. We had gone through all the proper channels we knew to get help and none of them worked. We finally resigned ourselves to counting the money we had and purchased one pair of boots. Michael and Lonny did get the clothes they needed to get through the winter. Michael and Lonny were so excited when they tried on their new coats and boots. They looked at the both of us with a big smile and said thank you. It felt so good to see them smile.

Within three weeks of eviction, Glenn and I decided to sell whatever we could to raise money enough to shelter us all. We feared homelessness and became especially concerned about the baby. The gas had already been 'shut off' and we were using an electric heater to stay warm. The back porch became our refrigerator. We prayed that the rats would not get into our butter and milk. Despite the worst of everything, Glenn and I continued to struggle with keeping the lights and water going and prayed for buyers. The next notice of termination was the telephone. We only had a couple of days before we would be without service. The telephone had become our lifeline to others who knew of our financial situation and the ability to get rides when we needed them. Now, here we were, within days of eviction and thirty dollars between us all. We began to pray and ask God for a miracle.

Apparently, He heard us. Just before the telephone was to be 'turned off', a property owner called about an apartment. The next call was from a woman who wanted to purchase all of our furniture and some other items we had for sell. She even wanted some French doors from one of the rooms. We took them off the hinges and sold them too. The only items we kept were our beds and the living room set, everything else was 'for sale'. In total, we made about $300.00. We thanked God for showing us favor. That night we went to bed as if we had just received a million dollars. We held onto hope that we would not be homeless.

A week passed before we were able to get in touch with the property owner who telephoned regarding the apartment. After repeated attempts at a nearby public telephone, I finally reached him and he indicated that he had changed his mind and did not want to rent to teenagers. Desperate and determined that our family was not going to live on the streets, I informed the property owner of our plight, but not quite in the tone he may have wanted to hear. I told him that if he did not rent the dilapidated apartment to me, that no one was going to live in it. I would make sure by calling the city and have the whole building condemned. He cleared his throat and told me I did not have to threaten him. In the next breath, he told me he would bring the key the next day as long as I promised not to have parties. I promised and instead of the next day, I instructed him to bring the key to me now and pick up his deposit. Due to our scheduled eviction within 48 hours, we compromised. The appointed time to meet the property owner was eleven o'clock that night. Glenn and I walked four blocks to meet him. I had told the property owner that we did not have time for games and he had better be there. He gave his assurance. I counted on his word every cold step of the way to the four-family flat. The property owner was waiting as he had promised. I gave him the $150.00 deposit and he gave me the key. Glenn and I stared at our new home. Yes, our new home was run-down and barely fit for anyone to live in, but it was better than the streets.

A SISTERLY BOND THAT CAN'T BE BROKEN

Moving in a New Direction

✦

Footstep Fourteen

When God grants a prayer, most times we tend to think of it as being the ideal dream and extremely unusual. However, God supplies everything we need in due time. We learned this lesson when we moved into the dilapidated flat. Despite the type of housing, it took some bargaining to make arrangements.

After a co-worker influenced some of his male friends to help move the few belongings left after the sale, we were on our way to a new home. We had to get the truck, and the men would commit the labor. We moved in on the day of eviction. The men said they were making one run, so we had to pack well. It was very cold the day we moved. The snow had fallen two feet deep. However, the sun was bright that morning, and for that, we were grateful. It helped to make the move easier with a bright, crisp day. We packed the truck as tight as we could and thanked the men for their assistance. Auntie was relieved to hear that all went well when I called her from a nearby telephone booth.

The gas and light utility companies came out to the new location on an emergency call. Since there was a newborn in the home and it being winter weather, we fit the emergency classification. The man from the gas company came up from the basement informing me that there was water surrounding the gas tank, and the antiquity of the furnace. We were all in danger due to the building being vulnerable to blowing up at any time. He was extremely concerned about supplying gas service and stated the situation required a report to the city. Notice of the severity regarding the furnace would probably condemn the building. He next advised us to leave. I pleaded with him not to send the report and turn the gas on despite the threat of an explosion. I explained to him that we had no place to go if we could not live here. He reluctantly conceded and told us,

"God be with you".

There must have had power in his words, because God was indeed with us that night. After his report of what was going on in the basement, I was naturally concerned about the other residents.

Frustrated and upset that we had to pay rent to be under a death threat, an idea came to mind. I began to knock on the other resident's doors. Introducing myself to each one and sharing the information that the gas man had supplied, I inquired whether they had problems with their apartments. No one held back how dissatisfied he or she was with the living conditions.

Edward, my father, had taught me well how not to continue to take abuse. It was clear that we were under 'tenant abuse' to the worst measure—our lives. We consulted the Landlord Tenant Association of our concerns. Upon receiving instructions from them on how to handle the complaints, we, the tenants, came to a decision. In order to have the complaint taken seriously, each tenant withheld rent to the property owner. After a few weeks, I personally notified the landlord that we would not release "another dime" until the building was suitable for living. He cursed for having let me move into the flat. However, we stood our ground with him and he began fixing up the building.

He started by putting new locks on the main entrance door. Then he repaired the doorbells. He provided paint to the tenants and removed all the water from the basement. The tenants were so pleased; they helped with other minor repairs in the building. Finally, he exterminated the building. After seeing and experiencing the enthusiasm of the other tenants and myself being pleased with his actions, the property owner became a very pleasant person to see and pay. All that was desired was a clean and safe place to live, once that was accomplished everyone's attitude changed.

The property owner would begin to respond in a couple of days instead of a couple of weeks for any tenant requests. I became the single point of contact for all of the tenants. After about six months, the property owner personally informed me that he could not have rented to a better tenant. He told me that not only did my efforts benefit the tenants in the building, but also made him a better businessperson. He appreciated the fact that someone cared about the property. The property owner would continually bless me with praises for taking care of my sister, brothers, and concerns of the tenants. In-group advocacy and the willingness to become involved in the process was evidence that I was moving in a new direction. Many friendships were gained by this new role for me.

Life turned around, it seemed, overnight. It was a good feeling to know that my brothers, sister, and nephew were now getting on with the process of living, as Auntie had assured me so many times. The boys graduated from high school, Diana was able to secure assistance to take care of her son. After Diana and Lonny started community college and Michael secured employment, I moved into my own apartment. Glenn, Lonny, Mike, Diana, and my nephew decided to stay together and help one another. Needing to fulfill my desire to go to college, I secured a full time job and supplemented my family when they needed help. It was time for me to step into my destiny.

During the ordeal of life changes from child to sister to parent for my brothers and sister took a lot of time away from Auntie and her children, Katrina and Eric. It was time for a reunion. God blessed me with transportation—no more city busses. My first car was a yellow Volkswagen beetle. Auntie, her family, and I would do many things together. We would visit parks, museums, or just relax eating junk food. It was Auntie's turn to go through tough times. In 1975, Auntie's husband left her and the children. It made her so angry, but she went on to realize that he was not coming back, so she moved closer to her sister Thelma. As the children grew and time went by, Auntie and I became closer. We began to spend a lot of time together. We shopped flea markets on the weekend. There were hardly any days that we did not see or talk to one another. Reflecting back on a promise Auntie made me when I was a young child, about dancing at my wedding with bells on, came up one day in conversation. Well, when my wedding day did come, (Diana and I had a double wedding), I reminded Auntie, and she taught me an important lesson—she said, "Don't let anyone *doop* you", you see, that's what I did when I said I would dance at your wedding with bells on—I am not doing it", with a raised eyebrow. That promise was real to me, more real than Auntie had ever imagined, however, I did not let her know,—the dance was not as important as how much I cared for her. Auntie seemed to be somewhat of a loner. She tended to be shy, except when it came to playing cards. She loved playing cards with a passion. Her favorite things were drinking cola, extra-long cigarettes, playing cards, and her children.

Auntie continued to remain in my corner in good and bad times. My husband and I have three amazing children. Auntie would take care of my three children as if they were her own grandchildren; from the time they were born, up to the time they entered school. She became a tremendous help to my husband and I as we learned how to become a family. I took care of her children too. When she began to have trouble with Eric, I moved him in with me to give her a break and re-focus him on his education. Auntie had two beautiful children whom I love very much and often have considered being as close to me as my own children. We were with each other when our children were born. It was hard to believe that Auntie and my father Edward were brother and sister. They looked so much alike, but behaviorally, they were indeed two very different people.

It took a lot of courage to make the transitions our family did during the years when Mamma and our father went their separate ways that did not include us, but God provided us with everything we needed. Family was a word that happened right in front of our faces. From the eviction notice, to the new place to live, we all learned valuable lessons of survival. It is indeed true; it becomes hard to hit a moving target.

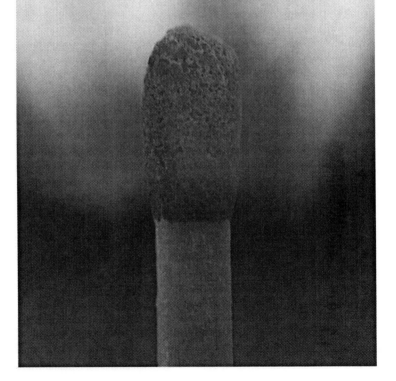

"Amazing Grace,
Thanksgiving Day eve, 1985,
Mamma Beatrice lay down to rest
and did not awake."

Edward, our father...died
October 2, 1991. It was over—our
father took his final leave.

Sweet Rest to a Lot of Things

✦

Footstep Fifteen

Several years passed before I could even think about speaking to my father, Edward. The heinous behavior he had developed in my life created such an intense hatred in me for him that it grew instead of waned. The thought of him repulsed me and ate at my soul. Mamma would repeatedly say to me,

"Denise, don't hate your dad or speak evil of him. God will deal with him in His own time. Your father will suffer before he leaves this earth and you will be the first person he calls. Do not reject him, go to him and the Lord will bless you."

In 1984, I could no longer deal with the hatred I had for my father and how it would eventually affect me. While sitting at the dining room table with my head in my hands, as I have observed Auntie do so many times, I was thinking about my father and entertaining the hatred inside of me. I opened myself up to the Lord and asked him to heal my hurting and take the bitter anger away. It was hard to move forward with the intense hatred that loomed in my actions and behavior. If my father had been ran over by a truck and died, the thought of going to his funeral would not have even crossed my mind. God and God alone is the only one who can remove this type of anger.

Within a few minutes, the telephone rang. It was my God-brother, inviting me to church. I had previously shared my feelings about father with him and he was aware of the effect it was having in my life. He cautioned me of the noise I would soon hear, it would be the sound of people openly praising the Lord. I told him the sound would be welcomed change of environment. We arrived at church just after services had begun. The atmosphere was just as he explained. The only time I had seen such open praise was when Auntie had taken me to church with her. I was very young then and did not understand why everyone was shouting. It was still some-what confusing even now, as I looked around. While observing the people and their actions, the warm presence of God, revisited me. It was the same feeling I had previously felt when I cried out to him in the dark trenches along the road to Aunt Catherine. However, this time, it was deeper warmth. My heart began to beat rapidly and it frightened me at first. Fear, because I knew it was God and I had not ever felt this close to Him. It was astonishing to see people baptized the same day and right after service.

My only other experience with baptism was when I went to church with "Big Mamma Ella", my paternal grandmother. Spending one summer with her at the age of nine, if someone wanted baptism they would put their name on a list and wait. I was amazed and wanted so much to be baptized. On my ride home with my God-brother, I could not keep quiet from my excitement of going to church with him. I went on as a child who had just experienced the most exciting thing in his/her life. I informed my God-brother that I would like to come next Sunday for baptism and asked him one question after another about the procedure.

The next Sunday could not come fast enough. I waited in anticipation of meeting God on a more intimate basis. When my alarm went off, I jumped out of bed, showered, and called my God-brother to see if he was ready. There was no time for anyone to pick me up; I wanted to leave immediately, so my God-brother gave me the driving directions. Impa-tiently waiting for him, (since I beat him to church), it was one of the most exciting days of my life. When he arrived, I grabbed his arm and rushed into the church. My brother Glenn was present as well. I proudly told Glenn that I was going up for baptism. He smiled. During service, I barely heard the sermon. My mind was on one thing—baptism. The end of ser-vice seemed to be "drawn out" and long. After the preacher ended his ser-mon, I stood up for baptism. My God-brother had to grab my hand and say,

"Not yet Neecy, wait until they call for the baptism, sit down", motioning for me to sit down.

Because I was not use to sound of people praising, it was hard to hear the right time to come so I asked my God-brother if it was time yet. When he said, "go", like a child charging to his/her favorite ride at a community fair, I practically ran. My focus was on immersing my life into that pool and not the procedure of having to stop and receive prayer from one of the ministers. They could not pray for me fast enough. One of the church sisters led me to the Changing Room where I quickly undressed and put on the baptismal clothes. Afterwards, prayer continued. I thought to myself, *"What is with all this prayer—just get me to the pool.* When I stepped into the baptism pool, the water felt cold, but I did not care. My heart beat with joy. The minister placed one of his hands behind my back for support and placed the other hand over my face. He then said,

"I baptize you in the name of the Lord Jesus Christ."

Quickly, the minister submersed me into the water and then raised me to a standing position once more. Upon coming out of the water, I began to cry freely. I felt a heavy weight leave my soul and an overwhelmingly feeling of joy. So overcome with joy, I nearly had to be carried from the pool and assisted back to the dressing room. When entering the dressing booth, I just sat there and cried. The baptismal aide came in and said that I would need to get out of the wet clothes. My crying had begun to release me and I could not even respond to the request. Between the tears and release that I had begun to experience, it was impossible to move. It was clear in my mind that I was letting go. Yes, I was letting go of all my pain and hatred harbored for my father. Freedom had arrived! After seeing that I was not settling down, the baptismal aides undressed me (as if I were a child) as I continued to reside in my newfound freedom.

Drying me off, they put back on my street clothes and shoes. They each carried me on their arms to another room (called a tarry room) where they told me to release all to Jesus. I was instructed to get on my knees in front of a chair, and start praising the Lord. Praise would begin by saying "alleluia" or "thank you Jesus." Further instruction was that I could say whichever praise I felt comfortable speaking, but was encouraged not to switch. I chose "alleluia", because God is worthy of the highest praise. As I began to praise God, I felt the strangest thing happen within me. My stomach began to knot up and I felt an overwhelming push from inside. The push began taking control of my vocal chords. Inside of me were forces greater than self will to make it stop—what was happening was phenomenal. My chest arched forward, my head tilted up, and my arms went out to each side. As this occurred, I heard myself let out the weirdest and loudest yell I had ever made or heard. The sound was piercing and sharp as in a horror movie. However, there was nothing horrific about what was happening to me—it was beautiful. After this release and freeing experience, I felt a newness come over me and a strong heaviness gone.

When I arrived home, I telephoned Mamma about my baptismal experience. She and I talked regularly about the Lord, and my receiving the gift of the Holy Ghost. She said that she wanted to come to my church and experience the joy she heard in my voice. We had talked about her coming to visit in December 1985 because I was due to have my daughter on the 20th. Mamma asked me if I would send her the song titled, Amazing Grace. She said the song made her feel good and did something for her soul. Many years after Mamma moved to Alabama, she joined a local church and received baptism. Time did not allow Mamma to receive the song or visit my church home; however, God knew all that was required.

Thanksgiving Day, 1985, in the wee early hours of the morning, Mamma Beatrice lay down to rest and did not awake. She suffered a stroke in her sleep. To me, Mamma died of a broken heart. Her love for my father and the loss of us as her children was so great; it broke her heart. Just the idea, of losing a family she had lived with most of her adult life, had to be a devastating reality. I shared her death with my father by a phone call from Alabama requesting he attend her funeral. He refused, saying,

"She's not my wife anymore; I don't need to do anything for her."
His statement cut like a knife through my heart. I could not resist responding, saying,

"Yeah, Daddy, but for nearly eighteen years she remained married to you and raised all of your children,—it is the least you could do."

There was silence on the phone. I hung up the phone and accepted his denial. Sharing the information with my siblings and God-brother Charles, who were with me, that he would not be attending the funeral, we continued to make the funeral arrangements. There was a service in Alabama and then her body transported to Macon, Georgia where she desired to have her final resting place. To honor Mamma's request was the least we could do—she had been the nurturer for us for so many years. There was no way the request to be buried in Macon would not be honored. My father's comment made me angry. For once, I had hoped my father would show some concern. We all briefly shared our dissatisfaction about his response and quickly got back to the arrangements as if we had not spoken with him at all. Rather than let his remarks take me into a rage as it had done so many times in the past, the new peace that God had given me caused me to feel pity for him.

As Mamma had prophesied, in 1989, Edward had suffered a stroke, and it was indeed my name, which became the contact in case of emergencies. It was time to communicate the news to my brothers and sister. Just before my father's first heart attack, we had begun speaking to one another. Despite all the selfishness and mistreatment by our father, especially me, it hurt us to see our father in such a weakened state sitting in a wheelchair. I had hoped God would give him one more chance.

As time passed, it became easier to think about the good times shared with Edward as a real "dad", like regular family outings to Belle Isle, eating fast-food burgers on payday, traveling to the annual company barbeques, and those pre-wrapped ice cream cones with the nuts on top. I wondered how he could so easily switch from being that "fun loving dad" to such a despicable monster.

Standing next to my father in the hospital room after his second stroke, I began questioning him. I asked why he had done all of those awful things to me. He took my hand and responded with this answer. He said,

"Denise, look at your hands—they look rough. That is my fault. I would often have you children work unnecessarily as punishment. All the things you are telling me that I did to you, I do not even remember

them all, but I will confess that I was a very sick man and I am sorry. Will you please forgive me?"
God had already given me a heart to forgive him.

After daddy came home from the hospital the second time, I would often pick him up in his wheelchair and bring him to my house to visit for a few hours. On one visit, I asked him if he would tell me in his own words, what caused the death of my biological mother, Elizabeth. His story went like this:

> *"We had some friends over from the military base and I began showing off a gun I bought at Sears and Roebucks. Your mother liked to kid around a lot and hid in the closet after all of the company left. As I opened the closet door to put the gun away, your mother jumped out and scared me, the gun went off, shooting her in the face."*

He said the shot was so close it hit her tooth and ricocheted to her brain. Continuing,

> *"I rushed her to the hospital, but she died on the operating table. Denise, the safety was on the gun, but the gun was faulty and I did not know it—not then. They arrested me and then released me after the hearing.* The hearing proved *that the gun was faulty and that it was an accident. Each time the trigger was pulled (while the gun was on safety), it dislodged."*

Probing further, I asked why he had not told us the truth. He responded that he has lived that night repeatedly, wishing it never happened, wanting to kill himself. It has been very hard living without your mother. You reminded me so much of your mother. You are pretty, petite, and smart, just like your mother. He said he did not tell us because he loved us so much that he did not want us to hate him. I would not ask him questions of what I remembered in front of my husband. The whole thing became a mute issue. Not wanting to cause him any more pain, I left well enough alone. Going to his side made it easier to remove the anger.

During the period of father's illness, I prayed often that God would deliver him. On several occasions, my God-brother and I would hold prayer with him. I could tell that daddy was remorseful for all the wrong he had done. He would often cry during our presence and ask God to forgive him. It was evident that God had indeed removed the painful hatred from me as I requested. I was with my father until he died October 2, 1991.

It was over—Edward; our father rested. The tortured evil that reeked havoc in our lives for so many years died with him, but the searing memories he left behind would spawn as a catalyst to help others not experience those pains.

Even though the forgiveness had occurred, curiosity and thoughts associated with mother Elizabeth's mysterious death still loomed in the atmosphere; at least for me. I began researching facts about our mother's death. It began with receiving newspaper clippings from California and Georgia. There had to be some information I could use to reveal the total truth. Thoughts of requesting records of the court hearing through the Freedom of Information Act were even entertained.

Despite our father, trying to explain what had happened, some things just did not add up. Why would his finger be on the trigger of a gun he was putting away? Only Edward, Elizabeth, and God would know what really occurred, however, it still bothered me. Realizing that nothing was going to change that dreadful night, I convinced myself to let it go.

Life continued second to second, minute to minute, so I too had to go with the flow. Wondering whether my father would have committed the acts against me had our mother not died nestled in the back of my mind. I just do not know the answers to the flood of questions and came to the conclusion that seeing dimly must be the way that God had planned it.

The heart of every book has a hero—the one that comes to the rescue of those in distress. Aunt Catherine was the hero in my life that appeared on the white horse to save me from the evil that could have easily overwhelmed me.

...IN THE CASE OF AUNTIE...

Woman on a White Horse

◆

Footstep Sixteen

"Happy endings" in fairy tales always have a knight on a white horse rescuing the beautiful princess. Well, in the case of Aunt Catherine, I was the damsel in distress and she was always there with her sword of wisdom and positive attitude to rescue me. This time it was a woman on a white horse that came and killed the dragons. The major milestones in my life began several eras of growth that would take volumes of books to convey. Nevertheless, to shorten the story, Aunt Catherine filled every conceivable gap of lost love and care in my life. This part of the book shall reveal a tremendous doctrine of power. From this doctrine shall come solution and help for others who may today be facing the same issue. The next pages will describe the physical deterioration of a woman, but a determined spirit of life. While the inevitableness of a disease can make one weak, the dignity of life does not have to suffer concession.

Aunt Catherine went through many life choices that caused the illnesses she suffered (diabetes, hypertension, and dementia), but now the choices change—we now must address even more serious choices. Humanistic regard is not a casual choice. Doctors and nurses take oaths and vows to service and care for the ill. We as family members, (or loved ones of family members) in their care have to stand in position for our kin when at they are at the hand of caregivers besides ourselves. We take a silent vow when we show our love for each other. The commitment comes through our heritable rights and legacies. Read the story of the fight that ensued for the rights of my Aunt Catherine. The unwritten doctrine of love between my aunt and I began legislature changes in Michigan State history regarding nursing home care.

In the appendix of this book is an actual complaint form, signed into law April 2003 (PA 3 2003, HB 4079). Place this book among your valuable and important documents. Thus, when the choice to place a loved one in a nursing (or hospital), you will have some recourse regarding their care and treatment.

SILENT SONNET-MELODY OF LOVE

It was four years later in 1995 that Auntie's health began to fail. Her work for the doctor in the exclusive Detroit suburb was taking its toil on her. Her blood pressure was constantly high and she had begun to take medication daily. I became very concerned about her health and saw a change in her mental state as well. Depression and melancholy came over her like a visible blanket. Common habits and treats of entertainment waned. She became less involved in her card playing. Even her daily care of herself was noticeable. She did not realize what was wrong, but realized she could no longer work and resigned her job. Auntie also became less jovial than she had been in past days. Often she would sit at her dining room table blankly staring out of the window.

Even the move to a larger place with more room and privacy did not improve the situation with Auntie. Her children, Katrina and Eric moved into their own apartments. Eric lived upstairs over Auntie and Katrina lived in an apartment approximately 15 minutes away. It seemed to make Auntie happy that her children had become independent. However, her elation was short-lived. Auntie fell back into a state of depression.

We all have visions of how we want our older years to appear. Looking at her life and the vitality diminishing, a marriage gone awry, and failing health must have made Auntie feel failed—something that was not in her personality at all. My heart ached to see Auntie in so much anguish. Doing everything possible to keep her well and fit would be temporal at best. As I did her regular household duties, shopping for groceries, washing, and bringing prepared food to her seemed routine for a short while. However, soon, Auntie became incontinent and required a caregiver when I was not available.

Taking care of Auntie was an honor. This woman believed in me, when sometimes, I did not believe in myself. She gave me so much of her wisdom and strength; it was as if she literally put her thoughts, ways, and ideas inside of me. Mamma's request to take care of Auntie would often sing in my mind. However, even if Mamma had not asked me to take care of Auntie, I would have considered it a blessing to be able to serve her.

HAPPY BIRTHDAY

The day was warm and sunny. It was Auntie's 65th birthday and about six at night when I arrived. She was sitting in her favorite spot in the dining room, however, this time she was picking her nails and seemed to be in a confused state-of-mind. There were no lights, television, or radio on in her home. Auntie always listened to the radio or watched television regularly, so it was odd that neither were sounding off baseball scores or wrestling statistics. Auntie loved the Detroit Tigers and watching wrestling. Remembering her enjoyment, even as a young child growing up, the excitement of these two sports was apparently her favorites. Yet, over the course of her settling, these were not part of her daily activities any longer.

When I came closer to Auntie, she looked up and said,

"Hello Ms. D'Neecy", calling me by my pet name.

"How are you today?"

"Fine, I answered in an upbeat tone,

"And how are you?"

"Oh, I'm okay—just sitting here."

Not falling into the dryness of her comment, I said,

"Auntie, do you know what today is?"

Before she could answer, I proudly announced,

"It is your birthday. Happy Birthday, you are 65 years old."

I sang the standard birthday hymn to her, forcing a smile to her lips. After reading, (the card brought to her and giving her a hug and kiss) we talked about old times. She said,

"Thank you", as we continued to chat away.

Even with smiles and chatting, Auntie did not seem happy. Asking her about her health brought about the response that she was not doing too well. Taking her hands into mine, I promised Auntie that if there was anything she needed to let me know and I would be there. Preparing her dinner and giving her another hug, I left with a commitment to come see her the next day.

The next day I left work, went home to see about my family and then left to see Auntie. Arriving at her home about eight at night I knocked on the door and rang the doorbell. After several knocks, I peered through the living room window seeing a lighted dining room. Auntie was nowhere in sight. She was not at the table or moving around in the flat. My heart began to race, but knew that she was there. I knocked on Eric's door, but there was no answer. Frantically, I went back to the living room window peering into the house and noticed Auntie on the dining room floor. She was pressing herself into the wall in an attempt to get to her feet. Yelling,

"Auntie, get up", through the window.

"Open the door—it's Denise, let me in", Auntie did not respond. Realizing that sometimes, disorientation takes over; I tried to get her attention. She appeared to be going in and out of consciousness. My heart pounded faster and I began to panic. I kept banging on the front window and yelling louder. Looking around for help, I noticed that the next-door neighbor had come out onto her porch. She was concerned about the noise. Despite her inquiry, I kept on banging and yelling out to Auntie. Attempting a call to Eric on my cell phone was futile. Finally, I went into the backyard and found a brick. As I began to thrust the brick into the front window, I turned to discover Katrina's boyfriend driving up toward the house. As he ran toward the house, I explained what was going on and he dashed back to the car, telling me he would return in about 15 minutes with Katrina, who was nearby at a friend's house. Those fifteen minutes seemed like hours. When Katrina finally arrived, her hands shaking, she unlocked the door. We all rushed in to where Auntie was lying.

Checking to make sure there were no broken bones, we picked Auntie up from the floor and sat her at the dining room table. The episode must have shocked her, for she had released bodily fluids. Katrina and I took her to the bathroom, washed her, and made her feel comfortable. It was clear that the family would need to develop some type of home-care system whereby we would all be responsible for Auntie.

We did just that, which assured that someone was with Auntie throughout the day and night. Katrina had the morning and overlapped hours. Eric would give Katrina relief in the afternoon, and I would come over and take of the evening hours (after school and taking care of my family). However, for me, a full-time job, family, college, and serving as a caregiver for Auntie began to take its toll on me. December 1995 there were some crucial decisions and sacrifices to be committed. My effectiveness in some of my roles became challenging. Yet, the position as Auntie's evening caregiver would not be compromised.

School was important. I was five months from securing my baccalaureate degree. My family understood and it seemed the only nonessential commitment became my job. Resignation of a corporate managerial full time job was indeed a sacrifice, but there was no other choice. In order to be close to Auntie, I moved into a vacant house owned by my husband and me (which was less than a mile away from where we lived). It was easier to continue caring for Auntie by shortening the distance, as I slowly became her primary caregiver. Continuing college caused me to move in with Auntie. My family began to feel the pangs of my absence. I began visiting them everyday to ease the gaps of time that I could spend with them. They would come over to visit and help with Auntie during the night. My children were young and did not understand the tremendous care that it took to keep Auntie safe and functioning.

An incident occurred one afternoon after returning from the grocery store. The front door was open when I approached the house. This was very unusual. Frightened that someone may have broken in or Auntie has left the house. Going deeper into the house, I saw Auntie sitting on her bed looking at television. Then the smell of gas wrapped through my nostrils. Entering into the kitchen all of the knobs on the gas stove were turned in the "on" position. It was clear that Auntie's dementia was getting worse. Options became worse. I needed a release to make sure that Auntie could get the best care-even if it meant more drastic measures.

The next solution was to hire someone that could be there when I had to go out on short runs. I hired a part-time caregiver for just that reason. To find someone to come into the home became a challenge as well. One applicant was intoxicated, another apparent victim of physical abuse, another did not appear to be taking care of her own hygiene. In order to pay an affordable rate for an acceptable qualified caregiver, the work pool for in-home nursing care proved to be expensive, but necessary. Later, the caregiver ran into transportation issues, thus extinguishing the option of a part-time caregiver. This left me as the primary caregiver once more. The next alternative was something that I had dreaded doing, but it was becoming inevitable—a nursing home.

Nursing homes were the places that family members did not want to send their loved ones to live. The conditions and history of nursing homes were not very favorable, but under the circumstances, there was no other way to assure Auntie's daily safety. It was hard to make a decision to put Auntie into a nursing home facility.

"Time came to make another one of
those 'life choices—heart
tug decisions."

Life Choices-Heart Tugs

♦

Footstep Seventeen

The choice to move Auntie into a nursing home did not come with a quick decision. Many factors determined that Auntie would eventually require nursing home care. We first began with applying through Medicaid for home care assistance. The plan was for therapists and nurses to come to her home. This was easy enough to arrange based on stay in the hospital after a serious diabetic episode related to Auntie's blood pressure.

Auntie's home began to look like a medical clinic. There was medical equipment everywhere. There was every type of machinery and/or gadget ever needed to take care of Auntie in her home. The house eventually had no other furniture except the medical equipment and her television. However, the arrangement did not give me the flexibility in my own life needed to continue in this mode. My young daughter and I slept on a mattress in another bedroom on the floor. The kitchen contained a small table. Through God's mercy and favor, I was able to get a washer and dryer to clean Auntie's constantly soiled clothes and linen. Even with all the necessary tools to carry out the laborious task, there was nothing to compensate for the physical, financial, and psychological pressures for me.

Time came to make another one of those 'life choices-heart tug's decisions. A family meeting with Auntie, Eric, Katrina and I resulted in moving Auntie into a nearby nursing facility during the summer of 1996. After choosing the facility, it did not take long to discover why families detest nursing homes. The strong stench of urine, unfriendly workers, and size of the semi-private room Auntie occupied convinced us that this was not an ideal location. There were very little or no activities planned for the residents. The overall look of the facility was depressing. Auntie, in her alert state was very active. She would express that she was bored and she did not like the facility. She also informed me that one of the workers hit her, but was unable to gain any information through my investigation. Quite unexpectedly, one of the workers did reveal to me that that some of the nursing aides do hit patients to get their cooperation. When I asked for more detail, she politely voiced that she had no other comments except,

"You had better watch out for your aunt though, because if she fights, they will fight her back."

Now it was not just the conditions of the facility, which would cause me to become concerned, but also Auntie's well-being. Upon hearing this information, I reported what I had learned to the Director of Nursing and requested an immediate release and transfer of Aunt Catherine to another facility.

The next location was located on Detroit's west side after a site visit. The interview and tour went reasonably well. Looking for cleanliness and a pleasant atmosphere seemed to be important amenities for Auntie. The building had a beautiful brick exterior. It was located on a main street surrounded by two-story single-family homes. The well-manicured lawns and flowers were evident of curb appeal. The porch was long and had sitting areas both up and down for both residents and staff members to enjoy the outside. There was a sign announcing the coming of a prominent department store near the home within a year. Auntie would love looking out of the window and seeing her favorite store.

With excitement and satisfaction of what I had viewed, I told Auntie, Eric, and Katrina about the new location. Within two weeks, Auntie and I went to make the final inspection tour. Walking with her cane through the home with an occasional nod of approval, Auntie and I informed the Admissions Clerk that we would be signing the paperwork. Once the paperwork was completed, we escorted Auntie to her new window view of her favorite store erection site. The window also allowed Auntie to be able to see traffic coming and going. Lately, Auntie enjoyed 'people watching', so this was an added treat.

The next scheduled event in the new location was a full physical by the medical staff. Auntie's results were good and she looked happy. We could tell that her new environment was acceptable. It was a great feeling to have Auntie settled in and pleased. I left her in the care of the new facility with a promise to come see her the next day.

SEEING MORE WITH THE LIGHTS ON

It was the fall of 1996. The concerns for Auntie's care nearly seemed as if we had found the solution. That was until the day I walked into the nursing home and saw other patients wearing Auntie's clothes. Then there was the incident of the missing walker and parts of her plants missing. The grooming of her hair and nails had deteriorated. Reaching one day to get Auntie a glass of water and welcomed by an empty pitcher, sent flags through my head. Initially, I had felt overprotective. In my effort to try to be fair to the nursing home I found myself completing a mental report card. The grade was failing. The final exam was the soiled clothing that Auntie was sitting in one day when I visited. Not to mention the countenance of Auntie's face—she seemed sad. When I asked her why she was so sad looking, she responded,

"I'm bored and they don't do anything with me all day—I want to go home." Comforting Auntie with a promise to talk with the staff about the situation related to activities, she relented to giving me the chance. The staff informed me that there were several opportunities for Auntie to participate in activities. Gradually, Auntie would join in and participate, and then some days she would not. The one activity she did enjoy involved playing cards. One of the nursing aides commented,

"She sure does like to play cards. She'll play all day if we let her."
Knowing that Auntie was doing something she enjoyed eased some of the disappointment, but not completely, there was more to discover.

One visit to Auntie found me in the bathroom washing dried feces and urine from her backside. An aide came into the room and made the comment that she did not know that Auntie could stand or walk. I questioned the aide and asked,

"What do you do when you help her with activities, you can't tell whether she needs attention?"

Her reply was a bit disarming, she replied,

"I just wash her in the bed and place her in the wheel chair, take her to the dining room, and then leave to do the rest of my work, that is somebody else's job to check them to make sure they are clean."

Fury was mild for the way I felt after hearing the casual tone of her comments. This called for talking to management and the social worker. Initiating a meeting, I posed the question,

"What is the purpose of a physical assessment upon admission if my aunt does not remain mobile or clean?"

Looking dumbfounded and starting to apologize all over the place, the management team appeased me with informing of the monthly assessment meeting. To ensure that Auntie was receiving the physical therapy promised at registration, I attended each monthly assessment meeting. It was disappointing to have Auntie in a nursing home only to get worse.

Regular visitations at the same time would not allow me to get a 'good picture' of what was going on with Auntie. Therefore, I decided to make impromptu visiting early in the morning before the posted visiting hours. Not only did I come early, but stayed late beyond the posted close of visiting hours on purpose. Looking forward to the staff saying anything regarding the extended hours, I made one of my famous visits early around 7:15 in the morning. Entering the room, my eyes immediately attracted toward Auntie lying uncovered, shivering, and soiled in her bed. Glancing around the room to see what was causing the cold chill, a window, halfway opened next to Auntie's bed, was causing her to shiver. It was winter and the air was biting and cold. When I alerted an aide, she said that someone wanted to open the window due to the heat being so high. A few weeks later Auntie had pneumonia, resulting in hospitalization. There seemed to be an apparent heating and cooling condition in the nursing home. Sometimes the heat would be so hot; it was hard to breathe in the nursing home. Even my children had made a comment about the nursing home being *stuffy*. The temperature irregularity led me to believe that this was not the first time Auntie had been in this condition.

Upon returning to the nursing home from the hospital, Auntie received a Medicare bed in another part of the facility. One of the staff members informed me that Auntie would receive better care in this area. Since the bed required increased monitoring and accurate record keeping, guidelines would improve care. I questioned why the difference between Medicaid and Medicare—my answer,

"That's just the way it is."

Assuring me that Auntie would be better off in this unit was little solace for long-term care. Upon expiration of the Medicare benefit, Auntie would return to the Medicaid unit.

Four to six weeks Auntie did indeed receive better care in the Medicare unit; however, it did not curb her sitting in soiled clothing and lacking proper grooming. Something was wrong. The next observance was Auntie's foot care. Auntie was diabetic. Swelling had begun to occur in Auntie's feet. After reading several medical reports, references that people and caregivers of patients with diabetes should pay special attention to their feet. Poor circulation contributes to diabetic foot problems. According to the National Institute of Health[1], simple daily foot care can prevent serious problems. Informing the aides that I wanted to see the doctor was my next step. It was time for Auntie to return to the Medicare unit, with looming concern regarding her total care.

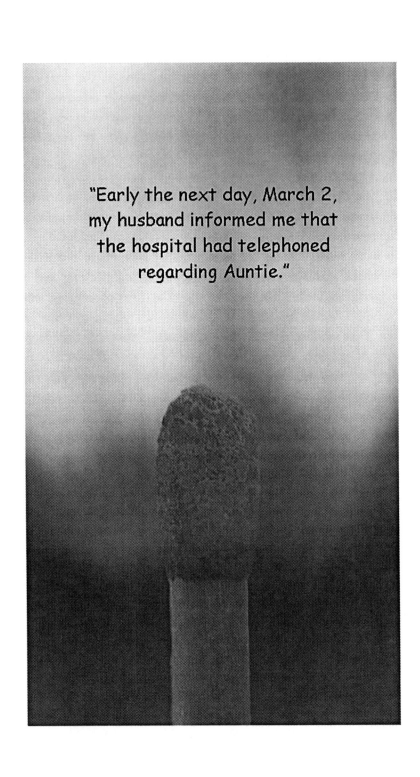

"Early the next day, March 2,
my husband informed me that
the hospital had telephoned
regarding Auntie."

Not Getting Better

◆

Footstep Eighteen

Just when I thought that we had found the ideal place for Auntie, the unthinkable happened. Total care for Auntie had worsened. There was a significant change in her care. It seemed as if complaining was useless. Nearly pleading to the Director of Nursing and registered nurse on duty seemed to no avail. Even when I requested that Auntie's attending physician look at the sores on her feet, acknowledgement of the requests seem to go ignored.

On several visits, we had noticed that Auntie's feet showed signs of tight-fitting shoes. The lamb's wool shoes had still not been used I had purchased. The Director of Nursing informed me that the lamb's wool shoes would replace the tight-fitting shoes. Despite the promises of improvement, once again Auntie sat without care, a strong stench of urine on her, hair not groomed, and again, her feet forced into the tight-fitting leather shoes. The lamb's wool shoes sitting in the closet area.

In an effort to force the issue, I had my son Curtis to take the tight-fitting shoes to my car to make sure the lamb's wool shoes would be used. We assisted Auntie to the restroom for cleaning and placed her back into her bed for comfort. There was an appreciative and satisfied look on her face when we finished. Curtis found it hard to look on Auntie treated in this manner. This woman had taken care of him and taught him cleanliness. Seeing Auntie this way was insulting and a disgrace. Storming out of the room, heading directly to the Director of Nursing office was little solace for what I had just experienced. I had security page the Director of Nursing and requested that the Director of Nursing speak to me immediately. After what was apparent avoidance, I returned to Auntie's room where my son had been patiently waiting. We kissed and comforted Auntie and said goodnight.

The next morning, arriving at about 8:00am, I requested again to see the Director of Nursing. Again, she was unavailable. Going to Auntie's room to check on her, she was eating breakfast. After letting Auntie know I was there and getting a good response from her, I kissed her with a promise to see her later in the afternoon. Later in the afternoon when I returned, I finally was able to speak with the Director of Nursing regarding Auntie's care and especially her feet. The Director of Nursing informed me that she had made notification to the physician and he would be in to look at her feet.

"When?" I asked.

She told me that she would contact me later in the day with the time of the visit and the results. Making a more specific request, she began to show visible signs of being upset with the demands. This occurred on March 1, 1997.

Early the next day, March 2, my husband informed me that the hospital had telephoned regarding Auntie. They wanted me to come there right away. He informed me that the messenger had not provided any details. Telephoning the hospital and wanting to know what happened was unsuccessful. It seemed odd that the hospital would notify me first and not the nursing home. The nursing had not contacted me. I was informed that the nursing home could not find the face sheet to Auntie's chart to contact me. It was through medical records that they had been able to contact me.

Immediately, I was on the phone once more contacting the Director of Nursing, who to my surprise was available to answer the phone. Frantically asking what happened to my aunt, the only response the Director of Nursing could supply was,

"I don't have all the details and just arrived in my office. Your aunt was rushed to the hospital because she was found unresponsive."

I then asked,

"Why didn't someone from the nursing home inform me of what was happening?"

She gave the same reason the hospital supplied—-the face sheet from Auntie's chart was missing. She hurried off the phone explaining that the police were there and needed to answer some questions. Staring into the phone in disbelief, I spoke into the phone—

"Police? Police? What are police doing involved in a—what is going on?" Hurriedly, she begged me off the phone and told me she would call me later.

It was apparent that this was not a simple medical alert and Auntie sent for a physical…something else more serious was happening and we had just received the alert. I immediately called Auntie's children. Explaining the situation the best I could with little information I had, we decided to meet at the hospital. Upon arriving at the hospital, and escorted to wait in a private family room, left wondering what was happening. A nurse came in and began to ask questions about our identities. This was an invitation not to only tell her whom I was, but also ask why we were called to the hospital. The gruesome details began to unfold. Calmly and cautiously, she responded with,

"Your aunt was found hanging between her bedside rail and mattress. She was unresponsive after CPR and is currently on life support and breathing totally on a respirator."

"What", I yelled. "How did that happen?"

The nurse responded that she did not know any further details of how it occurred. The nurse's apologies and cursory statements became mumbled phonics. I could not hear or see anything except getting answers to the many questions that were circling in my head. Turning to Eric and Katrina, I requested that they stay with their mother until I returned from the nursing home to get some answers. Suggesting to them to,

"Please keep Aunt Thelma informed."

Upon entering the nursing home, I saw several police. The lobby near her room seemed to have transformed into a crime scene on a movie set. Police seemed to be questioning everyone on the staff. Overhearing that two homicide detectives had even joined the investigation caused a shiver to go up my spine. The first thing that came to my mind was my constant complaining. Maybe, because of my complaints, a staff person had been suspended or chastised about Auntie's care and decided to do something about it. Could the Director of Nursing decide to take matters into her own hands and end my complaining? Had I been too pushy or demanding to drive someone to extreme measures? I began pacing the hall floor not knowing what to do or think. The nightmare stories I had heard about nursing homes hit home and I did not want Auntie's matter swept under the rug. It did not take me long to engage in a conversation informing the detectives as to who I was. Beginning a non-threatening inquiry, I began to ask questions regarding the investigation. The officer informed me that due to the nature of the incident with Auntie, they were treating it as a homicide until further information proved otherwise.

"It's routine Ma'am", he casually commented.

Peaking curiosity as to what "the scene" looked like, I glanced toward Auntie's room. Pardoning himself, he began to ask everyone to move aside. With all the movements, it made it easy to slip pass the officers, I was in Auntie's room before I knew it. Turning to face the inside of the room, I stared in horror. The room was a mess. Auntie's bed was nearly torn apart and turned sideways, which left little for the imagination. The covers were off the bed. Obvious signs of emergency medical equipment and participation lingered in the arrangement of the furniture. There were rubber gloves and wrappings all over the room, as if a frantic attempt at resuscitation had taken place. A patrolling officer made my evident discovery. He politely asked me leave the scene. Looking sad and very confused, I asked him whether he would contact the hospital and give me an update on Auntie's condition. Using his walkie-talkie, he reported to me immediately, Auntie's condition was critical but stable.

Returning to the thought of actual "foul play", I began trying to get the Director of Nursing. She did not respond to any of my calls. It was clear that escalation to the top was necessary. Evidently, bad news travels fast, the Facility Director of Nursing would not respond either. After calling the owner of the facility at his home, I spoke with his wife and asked whether he had heard about my aunt. She informed me that he was on the way to the facility and would perhaps contact me later. I left my telephone number and hung up.

It was clear that something foul had indeed happened. No one seemed to be responsive or show any type of concern. I grew impatient with the lack of answers and decided to take some action. I called Channel 7 News in Detroit, and told them what had happened. A news crew promptly arrived at the scene. During their interview, I told them that if my aunt was to die, I did not want the incident to be "swept under the rug." This sad state of affairs would not end here, no, not now—no, not ever.

The bill was in place…a place to be
moved into action!

A Higher Power

✦

Footstep Nineteen

After the news crew arrived, I was called to the Director's office to meet with her and the Director of Nursing. Neither of them would speak with the media. After sitting down with both directors, the incident involving my aunt opened for discussion. They explained that Auntie had been found unresponsive hanging from the bedside rail and mattress of her bed. An aide bringing breakfast to another patient in the same room had discovered her. The aide noticed Auntie's feet on the floor (opposite the side of the patient's bed she was serving) and called "STAT". The Director then contacted the night shift in my presence. She questioned whether Auntie was awake when she left March 2 at 7:00 a.m. The Director informed me that the aide said Auntie was up and sitting in her bed when she left. She informed me that the investigation was not over and would provide me with more information once they have it. I asked why it had taken so long to meet with me. She then informed me that it was because they were meeting with the officers, staff, and the owner.

After leaving the building, the news crew and I met outside with the information I had secured. Katrina and Eric called in to tell me (from contact to the hospital) that Auntie's status had been upgraded to stable. Not satisfied with the information I had received so far, I left and went directly to the police station and spoke with the officer in charge of the investigation. He and the other officers left the scene after notification of Auntie's condition. After informing him who I was and why I thought there might be foul play, he shared his findings that he believed it was an accident perhaps due to negligence and gave me a copy of his report. I left there heavy hearted and headed back to the hospital. Katrina, Eric, and I comforted one another and prayed. In spite of what the detective said, I still believed foul play was involved.

On March 3, Auntie was still on life support and not breathing on her own. The doctor said she was brain dead and was unlikely to recover. He would take tests and contact me later in the day. I did speak with him and he informed us that we may want to consider taking her off life support because it was unlikely that she would ever breathe on her own. On March 4, 1997, Auntie now removed from life support, closed her eyes for the last time. I requested an autopsy from the city morgue and was told the process would be automatic considering the nature of her death to determine the cause.

On March 4, I contacted the same local television station to provide them with an update regarding Auntie's death. The story was covered on the evening news as well as the following morning. My second contact was to Citizens for Better Care, an advocate organization for nursing home residents. I was instructed to contact the State to file my complaint. After contacting the state, Michigan Department of Consumer and Industry Services (its name at that time) via telephone, I was told to reduce my complaint to writing and send it right away to arrive in time for an annual inspection that was scheduled at the facility within a few days. I was appalled that a complaint was not taken over the telephone considering its seriousness or that the state had not been contacted by the nursing home at the time of my call. It seemed as if a brick wall had been put up to deter my complaint. I was not going to give up and transformed my complaint in writing and expressed it overnight as instructed. I also contacted the Food and Drug Administration (FDA) regarding my aunt's death. In early 1997, the FDA put out an alert regarding the danger of bedside rails and sent that alert to nursing homes.

While waiting for the autopsy report, a state investigator contacted me at work wanting to know why I was making "so much noise". She was making inference to "noise" as being the letters to everyone about complaints I had made relating to auntie's file. She said,

"There were no complaints documented in Mrs. Hunt's file".

Continuing the conversation with the investigator, I commented and questioned,

"Just because there isn't a complaint in her file does not mean I didn't make any,—and what about the sores on her feet?"

She responded, "There was no record of any sores on your aunt's feet, in the medical examiner's report".

Responding to the investigator, I told her,

"Well they were there".

She responded,

"Well your aunt is buried now and there is no way we can dig her up to see her feet, now can we?"

Furious at her tone and remarks, I hung up the telephone and immediately contacted the Medical Examiner regarding the autopsy. *He informed me that he had not completed the report and had not provided it to anyone.* He further went on to tell me that I would be the first person to receive the report. Within a few days, I went to his office and picked up the report. The report did indeed show that Auntie had healing wounds on her feet as well as marks around her neck (where she became entangled in the bedrails). It was apparent that the state investigator had lied. What concerned me most about her conversation was that there were no records of any complaints. I decided to do something about it. That is when the "Hunt Form" became a standardized complaint idea. It was named Hunt because that was auntie's last name. Secondly, there would be no need to hunt for complaints because a paper trail would have been established. The form was a multi-part document providing complainants with names of other agencies with whom they can file complaints.

Approximately two weeks after filing my complaint, I received a response from the Michigan Department of Consumer and Industry Services that they did not find any non-compliance relative to my aunt's death. I called it a "drive-by investigation" because only one person was interviewed and the findings were by far, a joke it seemed. Angered at the state's findings, I sent letters to my state and federal representatives, as well as the then Governor Engler along with a copy of my written complaint to the state. I also sent letters to state appointed members of the Department of Consumer and Industry Services as well as placed telephone calls. Nearly everyone I wrote or contacted responded. The Governor did not respond to me directly but contacted the supervisor of field services for the DCIS and asked him to respond to the letter he (the Governor) received from me. He did. I suggested the implementation of the standardized Hunt Nursing Home Complaint Form. The form would be a way to record complaints that would otherwise go unrecorded, and could help track complaints. He asked me to send him a copy of the form that I was speaking about and would get back with me. I also expressed my concern about the investigation being "coupled" with the annual inspection. He responded with,

"The state is short-staffed with regard to investigators and there were vacancies that were not going to be 'filled' due to a lack of funding".

I asked,

"Where does that leave those in the nursing homes?"

He suggested that I contact the Manager of the department, and I did. She informed me that the vacancies would not be filled.

I was rather surprised but pleased that I was able to get the Governor's attention. In summary, my correspondence to the Governor outlined some alarming conditions facing nursing home residents, particularly my aunt, and read that even with his status and money; was he assured never to face being placed into a nursing home.

The State was not budging from its position that the nursing home was not at fault in my aunt's death. I failed to accept this and pursued the matter further by contacting my district state representative. A reinvestigation of the mystery surrounding my aunt's death had to go up to another level. This time the pursuit would be at the federal level of government. Soon the Health Care Financing Administration (HCFA), known currently as the Center for Medicare/Medicaid Services (CMS), would soon know Catherine Hunt and Denise Bryant. A new investigation nearly eight months later found the nursing home (Oakpointe Villa) to be in noncompliance. They had violated four Federal regulations regarding my aunt's care.

"Yes", I said, feeling the aura of success.

However, the aura was only a vapor. The penalty of $100.00 paid by the nursing home was the nominal fee required to satisfy the noncompliance that resulted in Auntie's death. It was an insult, to say the least, that $100.00 would be all that my aunt's life would mean as a resident of a negligent nursing care facility. Nursing home residents and their quality of life seemed as much worth as fecal matter to the state or the facility. This was the conclusion drawn from receiving this "measly" sum of compensation in the mail. Some of the residents of these homes contributed, at one time or another, to society. They may have been the worker that made sure a family's food was safe to eat, or a social advocate, a nurse, or a myriad of other professional or service workers who rendered support on someone's behalf. The services others contribute during our lifetime are immeasurable. The time may come in some of our own lives in which we will require others to care for us. Thinking to myself, I shuddered. We cannot just kick the elderly or handicapped to the curb. Was I ever angry glancing at the check and thinking about the contributions that Auntie had made in her lifetime. The more I thought about it, the more I was determined to make sure there were changes for the better.

The next route would be through the legal system. In 1998, I filed a suit against Oakpointe Villa, whom Jules Olsman of Olsman, Mueller & James, P.C. represented. The legal basis of the suit was that Auntie's death was due to mere negligence. The lawsuit took seven years to settle. During the seven years, Auntie's death became nationally recognized. The complaint process in Michigan gained national attention in Washington and other cities across the nation. The United States Special Senate Committee on Aging, headed by Senator Grassley, (D-Iowa) held a special hearing on nursing home complaints to the state. In March 1999, an invitation to Washington, D.C. to testify before the Senate Committee allowed me to express my complaints worldwide. The event aired on CNN. Several media audiences also covered the hearing. I also testified before the State of Michigan House of Representatives describing my experience with the complaint process and how the investigation into my aunt's death had been inappropriately handled. An appropriations bill sponsored by State Representative Derrick Hale was before them to fill State Investigator vacancies. The Citizens for Better Care, Director Michael Conners, The Michigan Campaign for Quality Care Director Alison Hirschel and I were surprised and overjoyed upon hearing the favorable decision to fill 18 vacancies.

During the seven years of appeal, several other news articles and broadcasts reported the events surrounding Auntie's death. The grass roots advocacy organization, The Michigan Campaign for Quality Care, continued to push legislation on the standardized Complaint Form, which I had initiated. Finally, in April 2003, Governor Jennifer Granholm signed House Bill 4079 into law, which is Public Acts 3, 2003. Required use of the Complaint Form became effective October 1, 2003. Representative Gary Woronchak (R), Dearborn, Michigan sponsored the bill. To my surprise, Public Act 3, 2003 not only required a standardized form in all Michigan nursing homes, but also in all Michigan health care facilities. This was only the beginning.

Fall 2003, the opportunity to meet with several influential individuals in Washington, D.C. arose while attending the National Citizens Coalition for Nursing Home Reform's annual convention. The meeting was to request a sponsor for a national Catherine Hunt Bill. The bill would require a Standardized Nursing Home Complaint Form in nursing homes through all North America. The request drew extreme interest. United States Senator Debbie Stabenow (D-Michigan) is a co-sponsor of the Elder Law Justice Act, (a sweeping elder bill) and has made the "Hunt Form" one of her priorities. Her involvement was apropos. I am remaining confident, that God will allow a Federal Mandate of the HUNT FORM.

In 2004, the Michigan State Bar Association Elder Law Section and the State Ombudsman established an annual Catherine Hunt Award. The award merits any individual or group who performs substantial nursing home advocacy work the previous year. The lawsuit, working in the background, had been successful. The lower court ruled that Auntie's death was negligence. Again, efforts for success were blocked. We had thought of another legal victory, yet again, short-lived. The case transferred to a new judge who replied to motions filed by the attorneys of the nursing home's insurance carrier. In 2003, the new judge changed the prior decision and ruled in favor of the nursing home. He ruled that the case sounded in mal-practice and not negligence. Further, he ruled that we were barred from filing a malpractice suit because the time limit has expired. *He practically threw my case out of court.* We appealed to the Michigan Appeals Court. The court ruled by majority in my favor that Auntie's death sounded in negligence and not malpractice. In addition, we could file malpractice due to the original ruling of negligence. Naturally, the nursing home appealed to the Michigan Supreme Court. The Michigan Supreme Court accepted the case in January 2004. In the summer of 2004, the Michigan Supreme Court ruled in my favor and remanded the case back to the lower court ruling (civil). I knew the events were taking the form of a higher power. God would not let me down. He did not bring me through the trials and tribulations of life for nothing. All the glory belongs to God and my Lord and Savior Jesus Christ.

The millennium has brought a new beginning indeed to nursing home care. In 2005, the Catherine Hunt Foundation incorporated as a non-profit organization. The organization's primary function is to provide free (limited) and affordable non-emergency transportation to elderly, dis-abled, and nursing home residents for visits at any level. Enabling the right to maximize their quality of life

Eight years ago, the peace that I now experience did not exist. Now, a headstone on Auntie's grave shall commemorate the efforts provided in the fight for a Complaint Form. The actions shall take place September 12, 2005, in memory of all those who lost their life unnecessarily in nurs-ing homes through all America. The plan to place a headstone on her grave were intentionally delayed until there was some closure on Auntie's death, along with personal fulfillment that I had made some contribution to the betterment of nursing home residents. Public Acts 3 2003—The Stan-dardized Complaint Form, the Michigan Supreme Court decision of Bry-ant vs. Oak Pointe Villa, and the Catherine Hunt Foundation is my God-given contribution to the society of the elderly and disabled.

There is definitely more improvement of legislation and enforcement for nursing home residents required. However, now with a vehicle in place to bring noncompliance and negligence to the forefront, we must continue to keep the momentum for quality of life for the elderly. Despite our victories, there are several nursing homes and hospitals in noncompliance with Public Acts 3 2003. Elder abuse will be on the rise with an increase in the aged population. The HUNT FORM is a proactive and reactive approach to tracking abuse. It will take families, state and federal officials, and concerned advocacy to keep the issue alive and addressed. Rhetorically I ask, "What good is the legislation without enforcement?"

The Victory
Of
Catherine Hunt

Through time and stages
our body ages
and all our saved wages
is spent in phases.

We continue in Gods praises
while society rages
at the laws on the pages
that the politicians engages.

We have changed these outrages
laws that have enslaved us
and kept us in cages
which were not advantages.

Now we can be free
through Catherine Hunt's Victory
as we travel and see
that she has truly made History.

By Toni Curtis Fontana©2005

Then...

...and now!

We Came Through the Fire Together

◆

Footstep Twenty

Most of the time children imitate what they see adults participate in and do. There have been studies about mimicking and imprinting written in psychology books around the world. However, it is usually very hard to relate to the impact of the impression unless one lives through it. In our life, six children lived through imprinting that was not always ideal. Who does? There are no perfect people, yet, there are some better or worse than most.

Ernest, Glenn, Diana, Michael, Alonzo (Lonny), and myself came through the fire—together to survive and tell a story more familiar than we would like to admit. Somehow, the embedded ideas of a warped parenthood molded six sane and valuable children, now adults, by the grace of God. Our lives unfolded into a beautiful array of talent and a deeper love and appreciation of each other.

The eldest, Ernest, remembered our mother more vividly than the rest of us. He would also carry the most trauma and anxiety of the impact of the events that surrounded her death. Ernest wanted nothing to do with our father after the death of our mother. For years, he would constantly run away from home. Ernest started this life as a typical young boy, snakes, snails, and puppy dog tails, just like in the childhood rhyme. However, time and damage initiated by the accidental death of our mother left him bewildered with very little information. The emotional brunt of what he knew about our mother replayed a thousand times in his mind and eventually led him to seek escape. His route led him to lay his head where he could, including on the streets of Detroit. Despite talents of being a great sketch artist and poet, he could not find himself. Somewhere through the muck and the mire of our life, Ernest did eventually arrive at his time of stability. He married and has two daughters and a grandson. Became a widower and fell into his shell.

Our aunt informed me that Ernest was not the same after our mother died. "He was just not happy", she would say. One winter night after we discovered that Ernest might be living on the streets again, and with a severe winter storm advisory, Michael, and I went to look for Ernest. We found him. He was so excited and hoped that we would look for him and rescue him from himself. He was ready to become a productive citizen. Recovery from his pain is a daily struggle and he is making progress by giving his life to Christ. He is doing well and we are so happy to have him back in our lives. God again answered our prayers to restore our brother. We love you Ernest.

Glenn remains a close confidant to me as a brother. I will never forget the time Glenn surprised our father by getting in his face when he refused to allow me to attend a school function with my siblings. Our father was so shocked—even Mamma moved to the side. I thought Glenn was going to punch him. Dad allowed me to attend. Glenn grabbed me by the arm and we walked out of the house. Glenn coming to my defense was reminiscent of his fights for me in California when we were young. Unmarried and with no children, it is little wonder that he wanted to stay away from the ill representation given by our father. Yet, his genius, quick-wit, and technical professionalism stand high above the tragedy that occurred in our lives. As a successful computer specialist in the banking industry, Glenn enjoys his life without any negative implications from our father. He has struggles with himself and wants to come to God but thinks he must come without spot or wrinkle. Glenn, repent and come to God as you are—He loves distributing unconditional love.

Diana and I had a double wedding. Our sisterhood has a bond that cannot be broken. Not only are we natural sisters, we are sisters in Christ of the Apostolic Faith. She and her husband have six children and six grandchildren combined. We traveled the road of molestation together which sometimes haunts her and causes her to still sleep with the cover over her head despite the fact that our father is now long deceased. Even though he can no longer bother her, the remnants are difficult to discard as an old newspaper. A quiet person, she too has gained strength and moral turpitude despite the shortcomings of examples we had as children. Industrious and business-minded, Diana is an effective and well-liked retail-clothing manager and has been for over 20 years. During our early teen years, I often sighed while waiting on Diana to press every wrinkle from her clothing and coordinate colors, just to go outside and play. She turned out to be just who she is. When I need to coordinate colors and interior schemes, guess who I call?

Michael, musically and skills trade talented, married his high school sweetheart. He leads a busy life as a journeyman roofer. Active in his church as a student minister, a self made "handyman", he boasts five children and five grandchildren and plays lead guitar, initiated by the Christmas gift received from dad. It was again our father who Michael attributes to the shortcomings we experienced, yet, Michael's nervousness from stuttering and bumping the back of his head as a child on a couch have long been replaced with a balanced and stable life and livelihood. Michael contributes his healing to the Great I AM. Michael is a fine example of a father and a compassionate wise man. He keeps his family close to one another. I watch him in amazement.

Alonzo, (Lonny) has grown up to be a father of two sons and four grandchildren. He feels that he could have done more with his life, had it not been so rough with our father, yet he is thankful for his progress in life. As a service worker in an automotive plant and a self-made handyman, his marriage to his high school sweetheart keeps his goals high. Lonny was the youngest and usually got "his way" with our father. The best thing dad ever did for Lonny, he says, is to have given him a guitar one Christmas. Lonny is an avid bass guitarist and composer. Lack of funds and life struggles restricts the public from hearing his music. His wife has become a double amputee, which keeps his faith in the Lord strong. He says, at times, I treat him like a little brother and still give him a hard time. He makes me laugh.

Then, finally, there is Denise. My husband and I have five children and eleven grandchildren combined. This book, the Catherine Hunt Foundation, and my many victories speak for me. The abuse that happened to me in the past has become just that—the past. Through it all, I have learned to trust in God. Just as the scripture states, "To whom much is given, much is required."

We have been with our spouses for over 20 years. Our marriages have been both therapeutic and rewarding. Our struggle in childhood has given us the ability to handle the challenge of making marriage last. We remain very close to one another other and continue to support each other's needs.

Closure and communication has brought our family full circle. All of us as adults have discussed our childhood. We have faced the worst nightmares and stood toe-to-toe with destiny, but through it all, we came through the fire—together, by the grace of God.

Epilogue: What Does It All Mean?

People suffer many forms of abuse. Unfortunately, the abuse Auntie and I suffered is not unique. It has happened and is still happening to others. I pray and hope that individuals or groups in authority will begin to listen and be a catalyst for change. There are many people with silent tears because no one will hear them, believe them, or come to their rescue.

Moving a loved one into a nursing home or assisted care center may be as traumatizing as burial. For some of the residents of facilities such as nursing home and non-home care locations it is the first time away from family since aging. Not only are they entering a new dimension of life, but also their surroundings are drastically altered. Adding any other stress to an already traumatizing situation can be overwhelming to all concerned. It is hoped that the revelation and knowledge of this legislation assists your family and/or friends in making sound decisions regarding transitions of life.

We must all face the inevitable stage of life known "old age". Its entry need not be a negative force of life, but a very real and prepared phase of life for all concerned. When there is no education, vision, or systematic approach to a challenging situation, usually what is normal become abnormal. In order to prevent and curtail the transition, families and friends must be able to put their hands on the right organization.

Just packing a bag can bring a loved one to tears if not handled in the right manner. Mental preparation may be a route to make the transition clear and non-threatening, however, is not automatic. Just as our entry through birth to enter onto the planet, our exit must be handled just as carefully. Peace of mind is a lifetime pursuit. As loved ones begin to age and enter into the state of the unknown, there must be some pragmatic behavior by those which remain.

Not only is this a transitional time for the elder family member, but a transition period for those near and dear to them as well. "Sandwich parenting" is now a reality instead of some far off notion.

Public Acts of 2003
Approved by the Governor
April 21, 2003
Filed with the Secretary of State
April 22, 2003
EFFECTIVE DATE: April 22, 2003

STATE OF MICHIGAN
92ND LEGISLATURE
REGULAR SESSION OF 2003

Introduced by Reps. Woronchak, Anderson, Stewart, Rocca, Gieleghem, Woodward, Pappageorge, Phillips, Minore, Zelenko, Kolb, Jamnick, DeRossett, Richardville, Spade, Lipsey, Bisbee, Koetje, Kooiman, Voorhees, Middaugh, Hager, Ehardt, Meyer, Julian, Newell, Vander Veen, Howell, Ruth Johnson, Shackleton, Brown, Cheeks, Smith, Stallworth, Tabocman, Paletko, Pastor, LaJoy, Law, Brandenburg, Accivatti, Condino, DeRoche, Taub, Amos, Stakoe, Garfield, Caswell, Shaffer, Hoogendyk, Nofs, Wenke, Ward, Byrum, Sak, Nitz, Stahl, Sheen, Hulzenga, Farhat, Moolenaar, Gillard and Casperson

ENROLLED HOUSE BILL No. 4079

AN ACT to amend 1978 PA 368, entitled "An act to protect and promote the public health; to codify, revise, consolidate, classify, and add to the laws relating to public health; to provide for the prevention and control of diseases and disabilities; to provide for the classification, administration, regulation, financing, and maintenance of personal, environmental, and other health services and activities; to create or continue, and prescribe the powers and duties of departments, boards, commissions, councils, committees, task forces, and other agencies; to prescribe the powers and duties of governmental entities and officials; to regulate occupations, facilities, and agencies affecting the public health; to regulate health maintenance organizations and certain third party administrators and insurers; to provide for the imposition of a regulatory fee; to promote the efficient and economical delivery of health care services; to provide for the appropriate utilization of health care facilities and services, and to provide for the closure of hospitals or consolidation of hospitals or services; to provide for the collection and use of data and information; to provide for the transfer of property; to provide certain immunity from liability; to regulate and prohibit the sale and offering for sale of drug paraphernalia under certain circumstances; to provide for the implementation of federal law; to provide for penalties and remedies; to provide for sanctions for violations of this act and local ordinances; to provide for an appropriation and supplements; to repeal certain acts and parts of acts; to repeal certain parts of this act; and to repeal certain parts of this act on specific dates," by amending sections 20134 and 21799a (MCL 333.20134 and 333.21799a), section 20194 as added by 1988 PA 78.

The People of the State of Michigan enact:

Sec. 20194. (1) Subject to subsections (2), (3), and (4), a health facility or agency, except a health facility or agency licensed under part 209, and including a health facility that is not licensed under this article but holds itself out as providing medical services, shall conspicuously display in the patient waiting areas or other common areas of the health facility or agency copies of a pamphlet developed by the department of consumer and industry services outlining the procedure for filing a complaint against a health facility or agency with the department and the procedure for filing a complaint against an individual who is licensed or registered under article 15 and employed by, under contract to, or granted privileges by the health facility or agency. The pamphlet shall be developed and distributed by the department of consumer and industry services after consultation with appropriate professional associations.

(2) The department of consumer and industry services shall develop the pamphlets required under subsection (1) in languages that are appropriate to the ethnic composition of the patient population where the pamphlet will be displayed.

Michigan Department Of Community Health
BUREAU OF HEALTH SYSTEMS, COMPLAINT INVESTIGATION UNIT

NURSING HOME COMPLAINT FORM

Print clearly or type information on all sections of this form. Call 1-800-882-6006 if you need help completing the form.

RESIDENT INFORMATION		
Resident/Patient Name		Birthdate/Age
Date Admitted	Room #	Discharge Date (If no longer in facility)
Guardian/Resident Representative	Daytime/Work Phone #	Evening Phone #

FACILITY INFORMATION			
Facility Name			
Facility Street Address	City	State MI	Zip Code

INFORMATION ABOUT PERSON FILING THE COMPLAINT		
Your Name (if not resident)	Daytime/Work Phone #	Evening Phone #
Street Address	City	State	Zip Code
E-mail Address		

INFORMATION ABOUT YOUR COMPLAINT			
Date of problem or incident:	Time	AM	PM
Do you give permission for the resident's name to be released to discuss the complaint?		Yes	No

What is the complaint about? Attach additional sheets if necessary.
No. of pages attached: (   )

Your Signature:	Date Signed:

BHS-OPS-361a (Rev. 12/03)
Authority: MCL 333.21799a
Completion: Voluntary
Page 1 of 2

All nursing homes are required to post the name, title, location, and telephone number of an individual in the nursing home who is responsible for receiving complaints and conducting complaint investigations. Someone in the nursing home should be on duty 24 hours a day, 7 days a week to respond to complaints. You may wish to contact the facility representative or administrator before filing this complaint.

Sign this form when completed and submit it to the Bureau of Health Systems by mail or fax to:

Michigan Department of Community Health
Bureau of Health Systems, Complaint Investigation Unit
P.O. Box 30664, Lansing, MI 48909
Fax # (517) 241-0093

Other agencies that help citizens with complaints are:

The State Long Term Care Ombudsman
State long-term care ombudsman will help identify, investigate and help resolve complaints of residents of licensed long-term care facilities through its network of local ombudsmen.
Call 1-866-485-9393 (toll-free)

Department of Attorney General (AG)
The Attorney General investigates elder abuse and Medicaid fraud.
Call: 1-800-242-2873 or file a complaint online at
http://www.michigan.gov/ag/

Michigan Protection & Advocacy Service (MPAS)
MPAS can tell you who you should call to report abuse/neglect, help you file a complaint, or investigate an abuse/neglect allegation.
Call: 1-800-288-5923 or (517)487-1755
http://www.mpas.org/

BHS-OPS-361a (Rev. 12/03)
Authority: MCL 333.21799a.
Completion: Voluntary

Life Journal Pages
for
Your Family

Bibliography

National Institute of Health, pg. 119.
www.nlm.nih.gov/medlineplus/diabeticfoot.html

Suggested Reading

Nursing Homes: Getting Good Care There

[Second edition: 2002]
Sarah Green Burger, Barbara Frank, Virginia Fraser, and Sara Hunt, Softcover: $11.95 + shipping and handling

For a complete list of publications, please contact NCCNHR at (202) 332-2275 or visit http://www.nursinghomeaction.org

Complaint Form Access
www.cis.state.mi.us/fhs/complaints/onlineform.htm

View
www.catherinehunt.org

Email
rides@catherinehunt.org

About the Author

Denise F. Bryant suffered many indignities as a child and has turned her negative experiences into a fight for justice after the death of her aunt in a Michigan nursing home. She was born in Savannah, Georgia and raised in Detroit, Michigan. Upon attaining her Master of Arts degree from Wayne State University, she was honored with the Top African-American Achiever Award by the Black Alumni Association the year 2000. Mrs. Bryant is a member of the Manchester Who's Who of Executives and Professionals. She is the Founder and President of the Catherine Hunt Foundation, Inc.—A federal non-profit 501c3 organization that provides non-emergency transportation for nursing home residents, the elderly and disabled to help maintain or improve their quality of life and ties to the community. She is a long-term care advocate.

The author states that the paths she has traveled in life and continue to travel are not about her, but about God's love, grace and mercy.

978-0-595-36766-5
0-595-36766-6

CPSIA information can be obtained
at www.ICGtesting.com
Printed in the USA
FFOW04n1802040317
33085FF

9 780595 367665